# Becoming a Dragon

## Forty Chinese Proverbs

四十则成语　让你变条龙

# Becoming a Dragon

## Forty Chinese Proverbs

四十则成语 让你变条龙

For Lifelong Learning and Classroom Study
English - Chinese

*Written and Translated by*
Haiwang Yuan 袁海旺

*Edited by*
Marjolijn Kaiser

**BERKSHIRE** PUBLISHING GROUP
Great Barrington, Massachusetts

© 2019 by Berkshire Publishing Group

All rights reserved. No part of this book may be reprinted or reproduced or utilized in any form or by any electronic, mechanical, or other means, now known or hereafter invented, including photocopying and recording, or in any information storage or retrieval system, without permission from the publishers. Teachers at institutions that own a print copy or license a digital edition of *Becoming a Dragon* may use at no charge up to ten copies of no more than two articles (per course or program).

Permissions may also be obtained via Copyright Clearance Center, 222 Rosewood Drive, Danvers, MA 01923, USA, telephone +1 978 750 8400, fax +1 978 646 8600, info@copyright.com.

Digital editions. *Becoming a Dragon* is available through most major e-book and database services (please check with them for pricing).

For information, contact:
Berkshire Publishing Group
122 Castle Street
Great Barrington, Massachusetts 01230-1506 USA
Email: info@berkshirepublishing.com
Tel: +1 413 528 0206
Fax: +1 413 541 0076

Library of Congress Cataloging-in-Publication Data

Names: Yuan, Haiwang, author translator. | Kaiser, Marjolijn M., editor.
  | Yuan, Haiwang. Becoming a dragon. | Yuan, Haiwang. Becoming a dragon Chinese.
Title: Becoming a dragon : forty Chinese proverbs for lifelong learning and classroom study : Bilingual edition with English-Chinese stories and vocabulary / Written and translated by Haiwang Yuan ; Editor: Marjolijn Kaiser.
Description: Bilingual edition. | Great Barrington, Massachusetts : Berkshire Publishing Group, [2017] | Forty Chinese Proverbs, is a bilingual (English-Chinese) collection of proverbs, popular phrases, and two-part allegorical sayings, designed for self-study and classroom teaching. | Includes bibliographical references and index.
Identifiers: LCCN 2017018729 | ISBN 9781614720393 (pbk. : alk. paper)
Subjects: LCSH: English language—Study and teaching—Chinese speakers. | Proverbs, Chinese—Translations into English. | Chinese Literature—Translations into English.
Classification: LCC PE1130.C4 Y793 2017 | DDC 428.0071—dc23 LC record available at https://lccn.loc.gov/2017018729

# Table of Contents

Introduction by Haiwang Yuan     ix
Readers' Guide     xiii

## Basic Proverbs

**Mistaking a Bow's Reflection for a Snake**
*Bei gong she ying* 杯弓蛇影     3

**Playing the Zither to a Cow**
*Dui niu tan qin* 对牛弹琴     9

**The Fox Assuming the Power of the Tiger**
*Hu jia hu wei* 狐假虎威     13

**Adding Eyes to a Painted Dragon**
*Hua long dian jing* 画龙点睛     21

**Jingwei Fills Up the Sea**
*Jingwei tian hai* 精卫填海     25

**Heaven Separates from Earth**
*Kai tian pi di* 开天辟地     29

**An Old Horse Knows the Way**
*Lao ma shi tu* 老马识途     35

**Tricks of a Donkey**
*Qian lü zhi ji* 黔驴之技     39

**Pulling Up Rice Shoots to Help Them Grow**
*Ya miao zhu zhang* 揠苗助长     47

**The Dragon Lover Lord Ye**
*Ye gong hao long* 叶公好龙     51

**The Fool Set on Moving a Mountain**
*Yu gong yi shan* 愚公移山     57

A Man from Zheng Shops for Shoes
*Zheng ren mai lü* 郑人买履 — 65

Your Own Spear Against Your Own Shield
*Zi xiang mao dun* 自相矛盾 — 69

## Intermediate Proverbs

Dong Shi Mimics a Frown
*Dong shi xiao pin* 东施效颦 — 75

Learning to Walk in Handan
*Handan xue bu* 邯郸学步 — 79

Monkeys Rescuing the Moon
*Houzi jiu yue* 猴子救月 — 85

A Cunning Rabbit Has Three Burrows
*Jiao tu san ku* 狡兔三窟 — 91

Marking the Boat to Find Your Sword
*Ke zhou qiu jian* 刻舟求剑 — 99

A Fake Player in the Band
*Lan yu chong shu* 滥竽充数 — 105

Aspiring to Become a Dragon
*Li yu tiao long men* 鲤鱼跳龙门 — 111

The Man from Qi Who Worries About the Sky
*Qi ren you tian* 杞人忧天 — 115

A Horse Lost Is a Stable Gained
*Sai Weng shi ma* 塞翁失马, 焉知非福 — 119

Three People Can Create a Tiger
*San ren cheng hu* 三人成虎 — 123

Waiting for Another Hare to Come Your Way
*Shou zhu dai tu* 守株待兔 — 127

Catching a Cicada, Blind to the Oriole
*Tanglang bu chan, huangque zai hou* 螳螂捕蝉, 黄雀在后 — 133

Crossing the River in the Same Boat
*Tong zhou gong ji* 同舟共济 — 139

Sleeping on Sticks and Eating Bile
*Wo xin chang dan* 卧薪尝胆 — 143

Killing Two Birds with One Arrow
*Yi jian shuang diao* 一箭双雕     147

The Fisherman Benefits from the Snipe Grappling with the Clam
*Yu bang xiang zheng, yu weng de li* 鹬蚌相争，渔翁得利     151

## Advanced Proverbs

Using a Picture to Find a Horse
*An tu suo ji* 按图索骥     157

Seeing a Horse Whizzing by Through a Crack in the Wall
*Bai ju guo xi* 白驹过隙     161

Eight Immortals Crossing the Sea, Flaunting Their Magic Power
*Ba xian guo hai, ge xian qi neng* 八仙过海，各显其能     165

No Tiger's Den, No Tiger's Cub
*Bu ru huxue, yan de huzi* 不入虎穴，焉得虎子     173

High Mountains, Flowing Water
*Gao shan liu shui* 高山流水     179

Fiery Eyes with Golden Pupils
*Huo yan jin jing* 火眼金睛     187

Who Can Untie the Bell from the Tiger's Neck?
*Jie ling hai xu xi ling ren* 解铃还须系铃人     193

Thick Willows and Colorful Bloom
*Liu an hua ming* 柳暗花明     199

The Wind Ignores the Trees' Wishes
*Shu yu jing er feng bu zhi* 树欲静而风不止     205

A Promise Is Worth a Thousand Pieces of Gold
*Yi nuo qian jin* 一诺千金     211

A Pillow and a Pot of Congee
*Yi zhen huang liang* 一枕黄粱     217

Alphabetical List     221

Topical List     223

Glossary     227

Dynasties of China     230

# Introduction

*By Haiwang Yuan*

In English, set phrases and expressions can be called adages, aphorisms, idioms, maxims, proverbs, sayings, and even winged words—all of which have subtle shades of meaning. Students of English may be confused to learn that an "adage" can be defined as an "aphorism," which is in turn more colloquially known as a saying. They only grow more confounded to hear that a "maxim" may refer to an "adage," that can also, sometimes, be an "epigram."

This confusion is also true for Chinese *shuyu* 熟语 (idioms), a generic word for Chinese set phrases and expressions. *Shuyu* have subcategories, for example *guanyongyu* 惯用语 (a commonly used phrase or a colloquial usage), *yanyu* 谚语 (a farmers' saying or an old saw), *xiehouyu* 歇后语 (a two-part allegorical saying), *geyan* 格言 (a maxim, motto, or aphorism), and *chengyu* 成语 (a proverb).

*Chengyu* is commonly translated as "proverb," but the English "proverb" and the Chinese *chengyu* are not exactly the same. *The Merriam-Webster Dictionary* defines "proverb" as "a brief popular epigram or maxim" or an "adage," which it explains as "a saying often in metaphorical form that embodies a common observation." Close to those definitions, the Chinese *chengyu*, however, has its own characteristics:

First of all, the number of characters that form a *chengyu* is normally limited to between three and ten, but the majority of *chengyu* are formed of four characters, as the Chinese have always had a penchant for even numbers and symmetry (in language).

Secondly, most of the above-mentioned subcategories of *shuyu* can transform into an actual *chengyu* by adjusting their structure and number of characters. This is particularly true for the two-part allegorical sayings (*xiehouyu*). Unique to the Chinese language, a *xiehouyu* is a two-part enigmatic folk simile that starts off with a basic statement describing an actual situation and finishes with an unexpected twist, thereby creating a humorous or witty effect. More often than not, the second part of a *xiehouyu* acts like an answer to a riddle posed in the first part and is often omitted. This is very much like dropping "do as the Romans do" and leaving only "When in Rome…" in the popular English proverb. Therefore, Chinese speakers often use the *chengyu* "Eight Immortals crossing the sea" (*ba xian guo hai* 八仙过海) and omit the latter part of the original *xiehouyu* "each demonstrating his or her own unique skill" (*ge xian qi neng* 各显其能). Some other *xiehouyu*-turned-*chengyu* included in this book are "the tree likes it calm, but the wind won't stop" (*shu yu jing er feng bu zhi, zi yu yang er qin bu dai* 树欲静而风不止，子欲养而亲不待), and "Sai Weng loses his horse" (*Sai Weng shi ma, yan zhi fei fu* 塞翁失马，焉知非福).

Thirdly, a great number of *chengyu* can be classified as *diangu* 典故, a Chinese term for "classical allusions" or "literary quotations." In other words, a *diangu* is a story or a quote from traditional poetry or prose found in ancient books or records. As some of these quotes have become *chengyu*, their meaning is often only clear to those who are familiar with the content and context of the original source. Not all *diangu* are *chengyu*, and, by the same token, not all *chengyu* have *diangu* in them. In this book, we include predominantly *chengyu* that originated from *diangu* (we refer to them as "proverb stories"), because these are the most interesting stories for language learners or non-Chinese speakers.

Some of these proverb stories are about ancient people, as in the *chengyu* "sleeping on sticks and eating bile" (*wo xin chang dan* 卧薪尝胆), which came from the story of King Fu Chai of the state of Yue during the Warring States period. Some are about historical events, such as "three people can create a tiger" (*san ren cheng hu* 三人成虎), the Chinese equivalent of "fake news," which originated from an occurrence during the Warring States period when the king of Wei, convinced by repeated rumors about a tiger, began to distrust his favored minister. Others are about Chinese myths, fables, and legends. For example, "heaven separated from earth" (*kai tian pi di* 开天辟地) comes from a Chinese genesis myth; "the fox assuming the power of the tiger" (*hu jia hu wei* 狐假虎威) tells the fable of a fox tricking a tiger into fearing him; and "high mountains, flowing water" (*gao shan liu shui* 高山流水) comes from a legend of a musician being loyal to someone who is keenly appreciative of his talent. There are other sources of proverb stories, such as quotations from famous historical figures, as in the case of "no tiger's den, no tiger's cub" (*bu ru hu xue, yan de huzi*

不入虎穴，焉得虎子), a phrase uttered by the Eastern Han dynasty statesman Ban Chao.

These proverb stories are meaningfully succinct and vividly expressive. Therefore, judicious use of proverbs in Chinese writing or formal conversation is regarded as a sign of good education (and excellent language skills) rather than pedantic showing-off of one's knowledge or repetition of clichés. For this reason, the mastery of a certain amount of frequently used *chengyu* is essential to the learning process for a serious student of Chinese. Replete with summaries of prior experiences, quotes from famous ancient sages, as well as myths, legends, and fables, the proverb stories open a window through which any reader of this book can gain a glimpse into the otherwise mysterious and fascinating big picture of Chinese culture.

During its 5,000-year-long history, Chinese has generated innumerable proverbs. There is a proverb for almost any situation. *A Comprehensive Dictionary of Chinese Idioms* (*Zhongguo chengyu da cidian*, Shanghai cishu chubanshe 2007) has identified more than 18,000 *chengyu*. The *New Chinese Dictionary* (*Xinhua zidian*) includes 31,922 while the online *Chinese Dictionary* (http://www.hydcd.com/) claims to contain 51,398. With such numbers, we have to address the question of why and how the forty proverbs for the first volume of this book were selected. To be frank, the sheer size of the pool of *chengyu* made the selection a daunting task. Instead of reinventing the wheel, however, we built our list upon the experiences and results of numerous Chinese teachers and linguists, looking at their selections of proverbs for textbooks used in elementary and secondary schools in China. We then selected forty *chengyu* with compelling stories (*diangu*) to arouse the interest of anyone who picks up the book. Meanwhile, we admit that picking the "perfect" forty would be mission impossible. As for classifying the proverbs by difficulty levels instead of by subject or other methods, we listened to the suggestions from teachers of Chinese that we were in contact with via social media networks. These levels of difficulty are guidelines, and we expect teachers who use the book to apply the proverbs to their curriculum as they see fit. For this purpose, we have provided the convenience of an alphabetical list (by pinyin) and a list by subject. The *chengyu* and their stories, as well as the annotated vocabulary and sample sentences are all written in English and simplified Chinese. The bilingual nature of the book is designed to help both native and non-native speakers of Chinese to learn the *chengyu* proverbs.

While we hope that teachers and students will find this book instructive, we also hope that it will be useful to a wide range of readers interested in Chinese culture, whether or not they intend to learn the language. After all, reading proverb stories such as those found in this book is one of the most entertaining ways to begin to understand the collective psyche and consciousness of the Chinese people.

Haiwang Yuan is professor at the Department of Library Public Services at Western Kentucky University and a guest professor at his alma mater, Nankai University in China. He has authored and edited seven monographs and translated many books from Chinese to English. Professor Yuan is the editor of Berkshire's *This Is China: The First 5,000 Years* (2010), and a contributor to the award-winning 5-volume *Berkshire Encyclopedia of China* (2009). He also serves as a consulting editor for Berkshire's online resource ChinaConnectU. His book *Princess Peacock: Tales from the Other Chinese Peoples* (2008) won the 2009 Aesop Accolade Award from the American Folklore Society.

# Readers' Guide

Each chapter consists of an English language version of the story, a full-length Chinese story in simplified characters, vocabulary, and example sentences or short conversations. At the beginning of each story, the meaning of individual characters is given, the proverb is literally translated, the meaning of the proverb is given, and an English-language equivalent is mentioned, if there is one. For each proverb, we have provided some information about the background or original source, which can be found at the beginning of each chapter. Words and phrases that are included in the vocabulary list are underlined in the Chinese text.

At the back of the book you will find an alphabetical list of proverbs (arranged by pinyin), a topical list of proverbs, as well as a glossary of names and terms.

Explanation of grammatical terms:

| Abbreviation | Word Type |
| --- | --- |
| ADJ. | Adjective |
| ADV. | Adverb |
| CONJ. | Conjunction |
| EXPR. | Expression (often a *chengyu* or similar saying) |
| N. | Noun |
| ONOM. | Onomatopoeia |
| PN. | Proper noun |
| PREP. | Preposition |
| V. | Verb |

# Basic Proverbs

# Mistaking a Bow's Reflection for a Snake

| 杯 | 弓 | 蛇 | 影 |
|---|---|---|---|
| bēi | gōng | shé | yǐng |
| cup | bow | snake | reflection; shadow |

杯弓蛇影

**Meaning:** Being afraid because of imagined problems or groundless suspicions.

This proverb comes from the *Book of Jin*, one of the Twenty-Four Histories of China. It covers the history of the Jin dynasty (265–420 CE) and was compiled by Fang Xuanling (579–648 CE), a chancellor during the Tang dynasty, with twenty other scholars.

## Mistaking a Bow's Reflection for a Snake

During the Jin dynasty, there was a man named Yue Guang. He was rich and liked to make friends. He took great delight in inviting his friends over to drink and chat. One day, Yue Guang was entertaining a friend at his home as usual. After a sip of wine, the friend was about to put his cup back down on the table when, to his horror, he found a little snake wriggling in it. He was too polite, however, to tell Yue Guang about it. Instead, he gave the excuse that he did not feel well and left after saying goodbye.

Back at home, the friend mentally replayed what had happened, and the more he thought of the sight of the snake, the more scared he became. Soon he worried himself sick. Hearing of his friend's condition, Yue Guang came to see him and asked what on earth had caused him to become sick. At first, the friend hesitated, but after repeated prodding from Yue Guang, he finally let out the truth with lingering fear: that his illness was due to his fear of the snake he had seen in his cup while they were drinking at Yue Guang's home the other day.

As soon as he returned home, the baffled Yue Guang singled out the wine jar from which he had drunk with the friend. He shook it vigorously and peeped hard into the mouth but saw nothing but the wine. Pouring some of the wine into a cup, he sat gloomily where the friend had sat. He was about to drink when he became alarmed like the friend: a snake was indeed floating in the cup! Rubbing his eyes, he took a closer look and, with relief, realized that the snake was just a reflection of the bow hanging on the wall nearby.

Just to be sure, Yue Guang switched to different spots in the room and looked into the cup from various angles. After ascertaining that the snake in the cup really was just a reflection of the bow, he wasted no time in sharing his discovery with his friend, who recovered immediately upon hearing the explanation.

This proverb is a metaphor for groundless fear arising from frivolous suspicions.

# 杯弓蛇影

这条成语出自《晋书·乐广传》。《晋书》为中国二十四史之一，以唐房玄龄为首，作者共二十一人。该书<u>记载</u>了从265年到420年的晋朝历史。

  晋朝的时候，有一个叫乐广的人，<u>家财万贯</u>，广交朋友，经常<u>邀</u>请朋友到家里饮酒聊天，以此为乐。一天，乐广请一个朋友到家里来喝酒，当那个朋友喝了一口酒，正准备把杯子放到桌上的时候，突然看见杯子里<u>漂</u>着一条小蛇，心里十分不安，但又不好意思说出口。于是他推脱身体感到不适，提前<u>告辞</u>回家了。

  到家后，那个朋友越想越害怕，越想越别扭，很快就病倒了。乐广听说朋友病了，就前去看望，<u>询问其生病的原委</u>。起初朋友<u>吞吞吐吐</u>，不肯说出来。最后，<u>经不住</u>乐广再三追问，<u>惊魂未定</u>地对乐广说，那天在他家喝酒的时候，看到酒杯里<u>飘</u>着一条小蛇，受到了惊吓。

  乐广非常纳闷，回家后，马上把没有喝完的那<u>坛</u>酒拿出来，又是晃来晃去，又是仔细往坛子里<u>打量</u>，可什么也没有发现。他<u>闷闷不乐</u>地给自己<u>斟</u>了一杯酒，正巧坐在他朋友当初坐过的位置上，当他举杯欲饮的时候，也惊呆了，酒杯里果然漂浮着一条小蛇！他揉了揉眼睛，仔细再看的时候才<u>恍然大悟</u>，那分明是个倒影，是他那张挂在墙上的弓映进去的。

  乐广变换了几个不同的角度，确定酒杯里就是弓的倒影以后，就<u>马不停蹄</u>地把这个发现告诉给那个朋友。朋友听了，病马上就好了。

  这条成语比喻因<u>疑神疑鬼</u>而引起不必要的恐惧。

## Vocabulary

| Characters | Pinyin | Word Type | Translation |
|---|---|---|---|
| 酒杯 | jiǔbēi | N. | wine cup |
| 影（子） | yǐng(zi) | N. | shadow, reflection |
| 记载 | jìzǎi | V. | to record, to write down |
| 家财万贯 | jiā cái wàn guàn | ADJ./EXPR. | extremely wealthy |
| 邀请 | yāoqǐng | V./N. | to invite; invitation |
| 漂 or 飘 | piāo | V. | to float |
| 告辞 | gàocí | V. | to leave, to say goodbye and go |
| 询问 | xúnwèn | V. | to ask, to inquire |
| 原委 | yuánwěi | N. | reason, rationale |
| 吞吞吐吐 | tūn tūn tǔ tǔ | EXPR. | to mumble, to hesitate while speaking, as if hiding something |
| 经不住 | jīng bu zhù | | be unable to bear |
| 惊魂未定 | jīng hún wèi dìng | ADJ./EXPR. | still terrified from a previous shock |
| 坛 | tán | N. | earthen jar |
| 闷闷不乐 | mèn mèn bú lè | ADJ./EXPR. | gloomy |
| 斟 | zhēn | V. | to pour |
| 恍然大悟 | huǎng rán dà wù | V./EXPR. | to suddenly realize something, especially after pondering over it for a long time |
| 马不停蹄 | mǎ bù tíng tí | V./EXPR. | to hurry nonstop |
| 疑神疑鬼 | yí shén yí guǐ | EXPR. | to doubt everything and everybody |

## Examples

她不知道从哪里听到要地震的消息,整天杯弓蛇影,稍有动静就慌作一团。

I don't know where she heard the rumor that there would be an earthquake, but **she's so scared of the imagined danger** that she crumples into a heap whenever there's a mere stir of something.

现在的贪官污吏,整天杯弓蛇影,担心随时会被纪委约谈。

Corrupt officials today are **living in fear every day**, bracing themselves to be called in for an interview by the Committee for Discipline Inspection.

# Playing the Zither to a Cow

| 对 | 牛 | 弹 | 琴 |
|---|---|---|---|
| duì | niú | tán | qín |
| to, for | cow, ox | to play | zither, lute |

**Meaning:** Offering something valuable to someone who doesn't understand its value.

**English equivalent:** Casting pearls before a swine.

对
牛
弹
琴

This proverb comes from *Master Mou's Treatise on the Removal of Doubts*, a book of thirty-seven chapters and allegedly China's first writing about Buddhism. The "Master Mou" in the title refers to the author Mou Rong, a scholar-official of the Eastern Han dynasty (25–220 CE).

## Playing the Zither to a Cow

Gongming Yi was a famous ancient player of the *guqin*, a seven-stringed zither. Whenever he played, passers-by would stop and listen by his window, mesmerized by the tunes he artfully produced.

One day, Gongming Yi went on an outing, carrying his *guqin* with him. Engulfed in the picturesque scenery of green mountains and rivers beneath an azure sky filled with clouds like white sashes, Yi could not help but lay his *guqin* on the grass and begin to play. Soon he stopped as he realized no one was listening.

Looking around, he spotted a cow grazing nearby. "Well, why can't I treat the cow as my audience?" Walking over and sitting near the cow, Yi started plucking the strings. No matter how beautifully he played, the cow grazed casually, paying no attention to him at all. Frustrated, Yi sighed, "It's useless playing music to a cow." He decided to go home. He was preparing to put away his instrument when he accidently bumped a string in such a way that it produced a sound like that of a calf calling out. This alerted the cow, who looked up and around before going back to nibbling at the grass.

Gongming Yi realized that only humans could understand and appreciate the music produced by other humans. A cow could only comprehend the sound made by its own kind.

This proverb teaches us that when we do or say something, we must first know whom we are doing it for, or whom we are speaking to, so that we can get the expected response or result.

# 对牛弹琴

这则成语出自《牟子理惑论》。据说，这是中国第一部佛教论书。书名中的"牟子"即是作者牟融，一位东汉（公元25 - 220年）的学者和大臣。在讨论佛教的过程中，牟融讲了下面这个故事。

古时候，有个叫公明仪的人，是个古琴琴手。他琴艺<u>精湛</u>，每次<u>弹奏</u>的时候，行人都会<u>驻足</u>在他的窗前，<u>如痴如醉</u>地聆听。有一天，公明仪随身带着他的古琴出门<u>郊游</u>。到了郊外，看到青山绿水、蓝天白云，他一时兴起，把琴往草地上一放就<u>信手</u>弹奏起来。他弹着弹着，就停下手来，因为发现<u>跟前压根</u>就没人在听。<u>环顾四周</u>，不远处只有一头牛在吃草。"哼，为什么不能让牛来做我的听客呢？"他<u>遂移至牛</u>的附近坐下来，<u>款款</u>地拨弄起琴弦。可是，无论他弹奏得多么<u>悦耳</u>，牛都<u>无动于衷</u>，继续闷头啃着嫩草。公明仪泄气地自言自语道，"嗨，牛<u>毕竟</u>是牛，对其弹琴，又有何用？"说着就准备起身回家，可在整理古琴的时候，<u>不巧</u>碰到一根琴弦，奏出<u>酷似</u>牛犊的"哞哞"叫声。牛听了先是一愣，抬头左顾右盼了一会儿，接着又低下头去吃起草来。公明仪终于明白了，只有人才能听懂人的乐声，而牛只能听懂牛的叫声。

这个成语告诉我们，做事要看准对象。这样才能收到预想的效果。

## Vocabulary

| Characters | Pinyin | Word Type | Translation |
| --- | --- | --- | --- |
| 佛教 | Fójiào | N. | Buddhism |
| 精湛 | jīngzhàn | ADJ. | exquisite, wonderful |
| 弹琴 | tánqín | V. | to play the zither or lute |
| 驻足 | zhùzú | V. | to stop, to stand still |
| 如痴如醉 | rú chī rú zuì | EXPR. | to be perplexed, to be overwhelmed by, mad about (lit. to be drunk and stupefied) |
| 郊游 | jiāoyóu | V. | to go out, to take a trip |
| 信手 | xìnshǒu | ADV. | casually, at one's finger tips |
| 跟前 | gēnqián | PREP. | in front of, close to, near |
| 压根 | yàgēn | ADJ. | at all, totally, simply |
| 环顾四周 | huángù sìzhōu | EXPR. | to look all around (lit. to look around in four directions) |
| 遂 | suì | ADV. | then |
| 移至 | yízhì | V. | to move to |
| 款款 | kuǎnkuǎn | ADJ. | relaxed, slow |
| 悦耳 | yuè'ěr | ADJ. | beautiful |
| 无动于衷 | wú dòng yú zhōng | EXPR. | aloof, indifferent |
| 毕竟 | bìjìng | ADV. | after all, actually |
| 不巧 | bùqiǎo | ADJ. | unfortunately, accidently |
| 酷似 | kùsì | V. | to resemble, to be like |

## Examples

给只喜欢听摇滚乐的人们听歌剧，就像对牛弹琴一样徒劳。

Playing opera music to rock and roll lovers is as futile as **casting peals before a swine**.

他很偏执，跟他讲道理犹如对牛弹琴。

Talking senses to a bigot is like **casting pearls before a swine**.

# The Fox Assuming the Power of the Tiger

| 狐(狐狸) | 假 | 虎(老虎) | 威 |
|---|---|---|---|
| hú (húli) | jiǎ | hǔ (lǎohǔ) | wēi |
| fox | fake; to borrow | tiger | power, prestige |

狐假虎威

**Literal translation:** The fox borrows the might of the tiger.

**Meaning:** Assuming someone else's authority as one's own.

This proverb derives from a chapter in the *Strategies of the Warring States*. Historians generally agree that the book was written by multiple authors before being compiled during the Han dynasty by Liu Xiang (77–5 BCE), a government official, author, and scholar.

## The Fox Assuming the Power of the Tiger

Once upon a time, a hungry tiger was prowling the forest looking for food when it ran into a fox. The tiger snarled and opened its watering mouth. The fox was so frightened that it almost froze, but soon it collected itself and came up with an idea for how to get itself out of the danger.

The tiger was about to pounce when the fox quickly pressed its forefinger to the tiger's wet nose and said, "Hold it! You think you're still the king of the jungle?" The strange question dumbfounded the already puzzled tiger, for never had an animal talked to it so boldly and arrogantly before.

The impatient yet curious tiger howled, "What do you mean?"

"I mean you are not the king of the jungle anymore!" responded the fox with more confidence.

The tiger dropped its big jaw at the fox's shocking remark. Even more baffled now, it asked in a tone still carrying some royal contempt, "How do you know?"

"Haven't you heard that the Jade Emperor of Heaven has made *me* the new king of the jungle?" replied the fox, cocking up its head. "His Majesty ruled that all animals, including you, of course, should submit to me."

The tiger sized up the fox with a mix of disbelief and dread: the fox's entire build was no bigger than the tiger's foreleg, and a mere flap of the tiger's paw would smash the fox's skull and break its backbone. Emboldened with the thought, the tiger demanded that the fox show proof of its new status. The fox therefore invited the tiger to follow it and watch it inspecting the jungle.

Upon spotting the king of the jungle chasing a fox, though in a strangely unhurried manner, all the other animals took to their heels, all scared out of their wits. The tiger's astonishment was beyond description. It couldn't figure out why in the world all the animals big and small, which used to be its easy prey, would run for their lives at the mere sight of the fox. The thought of itself being dethroned and having to submit to the fox and, worse, the prospect of becoming the fox's food struck the deepest fear in the tiger's spine. It shuddered. When the strutting fox ahead of him paused and turned, he leapt a few steps back with a start.

"You know what?" the fox spoke. "I'm hungry. Now I will tear you into pieces and gobble you up!"

At this, the terrified tiger dashed away for dear life, leaving the fox chuckling secretly at the success of its deception. Knowing that lies never endure, however, the fox wasted no time in scampering away for its own safety.

Although this story seems to laud over a smart fox that protects itself by tricking a tiger, this proverb is nevertheless used as a rebuke to those who rely on the force of authority or the power of office to bully and oppress others.

# 狐假虎威

这条成语出自《战国策·楚策》。学界一致认为,该书的内容并非一人写成,但将其编撰成册的是西汉时期的官员学者和作家刘向(公元前77–5年)。

很久以前,一只饥饿的老虎潜行在森林里搜寻食物,走着走着,遇上了一只狐狸。老虎垂涎欲滴,呲牙低吼起来。狐狸先是吓得腿软,但很快镇静起来。狡猾的它对如何脱险已经胸有成竹。

没等老虎扑过来,狐狸用食指抵住它湿漉漉的鼻子说,"且慢!你还以为你是兽中之王吗?"这个奇怪的问题,让本就纳闷的老虎更加摸不着头脑。它还从没遇到过任何一只动物敢如此大胆、如此傲慢地跟它说话呢。

好奇的老虎急不可耐地吼道,"你说什么?"

"我是说,你不再是野兽们的大王啦!"狐狸更加信心满满地回答道。

狐狸这话让老虎惊得张口结舌,感到更加疑惑了。然而,它还是摆出王者的架子,依然用不屑的口吻问道,"你怎么见得?"

狐狸昂起头来反问道,"你还没有听说吗?玉皇大帝已经命我为兽中之王了,所有的动物,当然也包括你在内,都应该臣服于我。"

老虎上下打量了一下狐狸,心里又疑惑又害怕:这家伙身子还没有我的前臂大,一巴掌就能把它的脑壳击碎、把它的脊梁打折。想着想着,老虎的信心又回来了,于是命令狐狸拿出证据来。狐狸就邀请老虎跟着它去巡视森林。

动物们看到老虎不紧不慢地追着狐狸走了过来,也顾不得其中的怪异,个个吓得魂飞魄散,拔腿逃窜。老虎的惊骇无以言表,它怎么也搞不清,那些平时不费吹灰之力就能到口的大小动物,见了区区一只狐狸,竟然如此落荒而逃。老虎一想到被玉皇大帝废黜,要臣服于这只狐狸,还要被它吃掉,便感到不寒而栗。当信步前行的狐狸突然停下脚步而转回头的时候,老虎吓得倒退了几步。

"你可知道,"狐狸开口了,"我肚子饿了。现在,我要把你撕碎,一口一口把你吞掉!"

本来就吓得魂不附体的老虎，一听这话，头也不回地逃命去了。看着老虎奔逃的身影，狐狸暗自笑了笑，庆幸自己计谋的<u>得逞</u>。然而，它也十分清楚，谎言只能掩盖一时。它一刻也不敢耽误，立即逃离了危险之地。

尽管故事似乎是在<u>赞扬</u>一只聪明的狐狸，<u>临危</u>不乱，智斗猛虎；然而，作者却是站在兽中之王的角度，<u>抨击</u>和讽刺那些依仗权势来<u>欺压</u>别人的人。

## Vocabulary

| Characters | Pinyin | Word Type | Translation |
| --- | --- | --- | --- |
| 学界 | xuéjiè | N. | academia |
| 一致 | yízhì | ADV. | unanimously |
| 很久以前 | hěn jiǔ yǐqián | ADV. | long ago |
| 只 | zhī | M. | measure word for small animals, and one half of an object that is generally a pair (e.g., a hand) |
| 潜行 | qiánxíng | V. | to sneak |
| 垂涎欲滴 | chuí xián yù dī | EXPR. | to desire something, to hunger for |
| 狡猾 | jiǎohuá | ADJ. | crafty, sly, cunning |
| 胸有成竹 | xiōng yǒu chéng zhú | EXPR. | to plan ahead, to have a well-thought through plan |
| 湿漉漉 | shīlùlù | ADJ. | wet, damp |
| 且慢 | qiěmàn | EXPR. | to wait a moment, hold on! |
| 纳闷 | nàmèn | V. | to wonder |
| 不屑 | bùxiè | V. | to disdain, to think something is below you |
| 臣服 | chénfú | V. | to serve |
| 脑壳 | nǎoké | N. | skull, (fig.) mental capacity (brain) |
| 脊梁 | jǐliang | N. | spine, backbone |
| 拔腿逃窜 | bátuǐ táocuàn | V. | to break into a run, to run away |
| 区区 | qūqū | ADJ. | insignificant |
| 废黜 | fèichù | V. | to depose (a ruler/king) |
| 不寒而栗 | bù hán'ér lì | EXPR. | to tremble with fear, to shiver although not being cold |
| 得逞 | déchěng | V. | to get away with something, to prevail |
| 耽误 | dānwu | V./N. | to delay, to waste time; delay |
| 赞扬 | zànyáng | V. | to praise |
| 临危 | línwēi | V. | to be dying, to face death |
| 抨击 | pēngjī | V. | to criticize, castigate |
| 欺压 | qīyā | V. | to bully |

## Examples

自己有真才实学才是硬道理，光靠跟在领导身边<u>狐假虎威</u>是没有前途的。

To be successful, we must be truly competent ourselves. Following our bosses around all day and **using their authority to puff ourselves up** gets us nowhere.

小狗看到主人在身边，马上<u>狐假虎威</u>地对大狗叫起来。

The puppy barked at the big dog because **it was emboldened** by the presence of its owner.

# Adding Eyes to a Painted Dragon

| 画 | 龙 | 点 | 睛 |
|---|---|---|---|
| *huà* | *lóng* | *diǎn* | *jīng* |
| to paint | dragon | point | eye |

**Meaning:** In talking or creating any piece of writing or art, adding some essential words or a finishing touch to make the content come to life and have real power.

**English equivalent:** Adding a finishing touch.

This proverb comes from *Famous Paintings of All the Past Dynasties* by Zhang Yanyuan (815–907 CE), a painter and painting critic of the Tang dynasty (618–907 CE). The work provides a general history of traditional Chinese painting. Its author is regarded as the first Chinese painting historian.

## Adding Eyes to a Painted Dragon

During the Liang dynasty (502–587 CE) of the Southern and Northern Dynasties era, there was a well-known painter named Zhang Sengyao in Jinling (present-day Nanjing). His skill in painting dragons was particularly unparalleled. One day, Emperor Wu of Liang asked him to paint four white dragons on a wall of the Anle Temple. Zhang Sengyao finished the paintings in only three days, and the dragons he had painted were so vivid that it seemed that they could fly off the wall at any moment. Word spread fast, and people crowded the temple to see the masterpieces. They were lavishing praise on Zhang Sengyao's painting skills when some of them, after taking a closer look, pronounced that the dragons were lacking eyes. The onlookers were puzzled. "Sir, why did you leave the eyes out of the dragons?" they asked Zhang Sengyao. "Well, it may be easy to paint dragon eyes, but as soon as I do, the dragons would fly away," answered Zhang.

No one believed him, thinking that he was talking nonsense. So they kept prodding him to add eyes to the dragons to see if they really could fly away. Zhang Sengyao had no alternative but to pick up his paintbrush. He painted eyes on two of the dragons' heads. No sooner had he put his brush down than the sky darkened and a thunderstorm broke out. Then with a loud roar, the wall cracked, and through the crack flew away these two dragons. They soared on clouds and mist to the sky, leaving behind the other two dragons, blind and motionless on the wall. Now everyone realized that what Zhang Sengyao had told them was true.

This proverb was originally created to praise Zhang Sengyao's superb painting skills. Later, it became a metaphor for putting a finishing touch to an article, a speech, or an artistic work to make it more vivid and impressive.

# 画龙点睛

这条成语出自唐代画家、绘画理论家张彦远（815-907年）的《历代名画记》。《历代名画记》是中国第一部绘画通史著作，张彦远被称为国画历史学家的鼻祖。

在南北朝的梁朝时期，今日南京的金陵有位著名的大画家叫张僧繇，他能把龙画得出神入化。一天，梁武帝要张僧繇在安乐寺的墙壁上画四条白龙。张僧繇仅用三天的时间就画好了。龙画得活灵活现，跃然墙上。人们听说后，纷纷来到寺庙观看，对张僧繇的画功赞叹不已。可是，当人们仔细观看的时候，却发现四条龙都没有眼睛。人们不解地问大画家张僧繇："先生，您的龙怎么都不画上眼睛呢？"张僧繇解释说："画眼睛倒不难，只怕一画上，龙就会飞走的！"大家都不信，认为他胡说，便坚持要他把眼睛画上，看看龙到底会不会飞走。张僧繇没有办法，只好硬着头皮拿起画笔，给其中两条龙点画上了眼睛。他刚一放下画笔，天就黑暗下来，不久便雷雨大作，接着只听得"轰"的一声巨响，墙壁裂了开来，上边那两条画了眼睛的白龙已经腾云驾雾，飞到天上去了，而那两条没有点睛的白龙仍然一动不动地留在墙壁上。人们这才相信了张僧繇所说的话。

这条成语本来是赞美画家张僧繇精湛的绘画技艺的。后比喻写文章、讲话或进行艺术创作时，在关键的地方加上精彩的一笔，使内容更加生动传神。

## Vocabulary

| Characters | Pinyin | Word Type | Translation |
| --- | --- | --- | --- |
| 鼻祖 | bízǔ | N. | originator, the "father" of a tradition |
| 出神入化 | chū shén rù huà | ADJ. | achieving the acme of perfection |
| 活灵活现 | huó líng huó xiàn | ADJ. | vivid, lifelike |
| 跃然 | yuèrán | V. | to stand out, to appear as a lively image |
| 赞叹 | zàntàn | V. | to marvel at |
| 不已 | bùyǐ | ADV. | endlessly, constantly |
| 不解 | bù jiě | ADJ./ADV. | confused; in confusion |
| 胡说 | húshuō | V. | to talk nonsense |
| 坚持 | jiānchí | V. | to persist, to insist on |
| 硬着头皮 | yìng zhe tóu pí | EXPR. | to get ready to summon up the courage to do something |
| 黑暗 | hēi'àn | ADJ. | dark, darkness |
| 轰 | hōng | V./ONOM. | to rumble; boom, sound of an explosion |
| 腾云驾雾 | téng yún jià wù | V. | to climb up the clouds and ride the mist |
| 赞美 | zànměi | V. | to praise, to admire |
| 精湛 | jīngzhàn | ADJ. | skillful |
| 关键 | guānjiàn | N. | the crucial point |

## Examples

原本不生动的文章，被老师简略增删几句，竟使全文色彩焕然一新。真可以说是"<u>画龙点睛</u>"之笔。

An originally uninteresting article has taken on new life after the teacher's slight editing, a truly **magical finishing touch**.

把圣诞树装点好以后，在其顶端安放上一颗星，起到了<u>画龙点睛</u>的作用。

Placing a star on this decorated Christmas tree is **like putting the finishing touches** on a masterpiece.

# Jingwei Fills Up the Sea

| 精卫 | 填 | 海 |
|---|---|---|
| Jīngwèi | tián | hǎi |
| Jingwei (bird) | to fill | sea |

精卫填海

**Meaning:** Bent on achieving one's goal despite daunting difficulties.

This proverb comes from a story in the *Classic of Mountains and Seas*. Believed to have been compiled between the fourth century BCE and the early Han dynasty (206 BCE–220 CE) by unknown authors, the book is a mythic geographical and cultural account of China prior to the Qin dynasty (221–207 BCE).

## Jingwei Fills Up the Sea

In a thick forest on Mount Fajiu, there lived a bird named Jingwei, whose name came from its call that sounded like "jingwei-jingwei." The bird had a colorful crown, a white beak, and red legs. It was the incarnation of Emperor Yan's youngest daughter, Nüwa, which literally means "girl." She had gone to swim in the East Sea but never resurfaced. The spirit of the drowned princess had turned into this Jingwei bird. To avenge her death, Jingwei attempted the impossible: she picked up one pebble after another and one twig after the other from Mount Fajiu and dropped them into the East Sea. Flying back and forth, she tried to fill up the ocean. She flew nonstop until she died of exhaustion.

This proverb describes the spirit of determination that leads one to attempt seemingly unachievable goals, even at great cost to one's life and wellbeing.

# 精卫填海

这则成语出自《山海经》，其成书时间大约为公元前四世纪至汉代初期（公元前206‑220年），作者不详。《山海经》是一部以神话为形式，记述先秦（公元前221‑207年）中国地理和文化的典籍。

  在发鸠山一片茂密的森林里，曾经栖息着一只小鸟，叫精卫，因其"精卫、精卫"的叫声而得名。小鸟花冠、白喙、红脚，本来是炎帝最年幼的女儿，叫女娃。当初，她去东海游泳，结果再也没有浮出水面。这位被大海吞噬的小公主，其灵魂幻化成这只精卫鸟。为给自己复仇，她试图做一件谁也做不到的事情：从发鸠山衔来石子和树枝，然后把它们丢进东海，将其填起来。她不停地飞来飞去，最终因体力不支而死去。

## Vocabulary

| Characters | Pinyin | Word Type | Translation |
| --- | --- | --- | --- |
| 精卫 | Jīngwèi | PN. | Jīngwèi (name of a legendary bird) |
| 填 | tián | V. | to fill |
| 茂密 | màomì | ADJ. | thick; dense |
| 栖息 | qīxī | V. | to perch |
| 冠 | guān | N. | crown; comb (of bird) |
| 喙 | huì | N. | beak |
| 炎帝 | Yán Dì | PN. | Emperor Yan, one of the five primordial rulers in Chinese history |
| 吞噬 | tūnshì | V. | to swallow; to engulf |
| 灵魂 | línghún | N. | spirit, soul |
| 幻化 | huànhuà | V. | to transform; to incarnate |
| 复仇 | fùchóu | V. | to revenge; to avenge |
| 衔 | xián | V. | (of animal or bird) to hold in the mouth |
| 体力不支 | tǐlì bù zhī | V. | to collapse; to be over exhausted |

## Examples

二战时期，中国军民本着<u>精卫填海</u>的精神，把日本侵略者赶出了中国。

During WWII, the Chinese people and their armies **fought dauntlessly** and drove the Japanese aggressors out of their land.

如果要想实现自己的梦想，就要有<u>精卫填海</u>的精神。

To realize one's dream, one must have a drive like Jingwei who tried to fill up the sea.

# Heaven Separates from Earth

| 开 | 天 | 辟 | 地 |
|---|---|---|---|
| kāi | tiān | pì | dì |
| to open | sky, heaven | to open | earth |

**Literal translation:** Opening sky and opening earth.

**Meaning:** Ground-breaking; since the dawn of time.

This proverb comes from a creation myth that first appeared in *The Historical Records of the Three Sovereigns and Five Emperors* written by Xu Zheng, a historian in the state of Wu during the Three Kingdoms period (220–265 CE). The story was cited by Ouyang Xun (557–641 CE), a Confucian scholar and calligrapher of the early Tang dynasty, in his encyclopedic work *Collection of Literature by Category*.

## Heaven Separates from Earth

In the beginning, there was nothing in the universe but a cosmic egg of formless chaos, in which Pangu, the creator of the world, was born. After about 18,000 years, the egg-white-like *yang* (the bright, positive, masculine principle in Chinese dualistic cosmology) began to form into what is known as the sky while the yolk-like *yin* (the dark, negative, feminine principle) coalesced into what is now known as the earth. Inside this ever-expanding cosmic egg of chaos, Pangu was growing nine times each day, adding ten feet each time. Meanwhile, the thicknesses of the sky and the earth were increasing at the same rate. After another 18,000 years, the egg reached its ultimate size and stopped expanding. Pangu then broke the egg shell with a swing of his giant axe. He set his feet upon the earth of *yin* and carried the sky of *yang* upon his head. He stood 90,000 feet tall to prevent the two from coming together. There he stood for another 18,000 years, keeping the sky and the earth separated.

Finally, Pangu became so exhausted that he dropped dead. His last breath became the wind, mist, and clouds. His voice became the thunder; his blood and body fluids became rivers; and his sweat became the rain and dew. His torso and limbs became the five mountains acting as pillars supporting the sky in the center and the four corners of the earth. His left eye turned into the sun, his right eye the moon, and his facial hair the other heavenly bodies. His muscles became the land and soil; his body hair, the plants and trees; his bones and marrows, the minerals and precious stones; and the parasites in and on his body, the living creatures on the earth.

This proverb is often used to speak of something unprecedented or epoch-making. It also acts as an adverb meaning "since the dawn of time" or "since the beginning of history."

# 开天辟地

这条成语源自三国时期东吴历史学家徐整（公元220‐280年）在其《三五历记》中讲述的一个神话故事。唐代儒家学者、大书法家欧阳询，在其撰写的类书《艺文类聚》中引用了这个神话故事。

　　天地开辟之前，混沌的宇宙形如巨蛋，蛋中生有盘古。过了一万八千年，在蛋形的混沌宇宙中，阳性而又清爽的物质，升华为天空；阴性而又浑浊的物质，则沉淀为大地。阴阳，是中华文化的精髓，是其两分法宇宙观中一个相辅相成的概念。在不断膨胀的巨蛋中，盘古每天都会生长九次，长出一丈之高。与此同时，天和地每天也各增一丈之厚。又过了一万八千年，蛋形宇宙膨胀到了极限，于是盘古就手挥巨斧，劈开了蛋壳，其九千丈高的身躯，耸在天地之间，防止天地重新合并。他一站就是一万八千年，直到天地永远分开。此时的他已经精疲力尽，倒地而亡。死亡时，他呼出的最后一口气变成了风、雾和云；他的声音变成了雷电；他的身躯和四肢变成了五座大山，一座立于大地的中央，其余矗立在大地的四个角落，成为擎天巨柱。他的左眼化作太阳，右眼化作月亮；他脸上的汗毛化作星辰；他的血液和体液化作江河；他的汗水化作雨露；他的肌肉化作土地；他的体毛化作树木；他的骨头和骨髓化作矿物和宝石；就连他身上和身体里的寄生虫，也化作了大地上的生物。

　　该成语常指空前或划时代的事物；或用作时间状语，往往在其前面加上主语"盘古"，表示"自古以来"的意思。

## Vocabulary

| Characters | Pinyin | Word Type | Translation |
|---|---|---|---|
| 神话 | shénhuà | N. | myth, fairytale |
| 引用 | yǐnyòng | V. | to cite, to quote |
| 混沌 | hùndùn | N. | primal chaos |
| 宇宙 | yǔzhòu | N. | universe, cosmos |
| 升华 | shēnghuá | V. | to rise to a higher level, so sublimate |
| 沉淀 | chéndiàn | V. | to settle in |
| 精髓 | jīngsuǐ | N. | gist |
| 两分法 | liǎngfēnfǎ | EXPR. | dualistic, one divides into two |
| 宇宙观 | yǔzhòuguān | N | world view, cosmology |
| 相辅相成 | xiāng fǔ xiāng chéng | ADJ., V. | complementary; to complement |
| 膨胀 | péngzhàng | V. | to expand, to swell up |
| 极限 | jíxiàn | N. | limit, extreme |
| 挥 | huī | V. | to wave, to scatter |
| 蛋壳 | dànké | N. | eggshell |
| 耸 | sǒng | V. | to raise up, to shrug |
| 防止 | fángzhǐ | V. | to guard against, to prevent |
| 合并 | hébìng | V. | to merge |
| 精疲力尽 | jīng pí lì jìn | ADJ. | exhausted |
| 矗立 | chùlì | V. | to stand, especially used to describe mountains or statues |
| 擎 | qíng | V. | to raise |
| 矿物 | kuàngwù | N. | mineral |
| 寄生虫 | jìshēngchóng | N. | parasite |

## Examples

中国量子卫星的发射，是一件<u>开天辟地</u>的大事。

It is **an epoch-making** event that the Chinese launched its quantum satellite.

一切发明总会有其根源,自盘古<u>开天辟地</u>以来，任何东西都不会无中生有：就连今天的飞机在很大程度上也和鸟相关。

All inventions have their roots in something else; for **since the dawn of history**, nothing has been created out of nothing. Even the airplane, for example, is closely related to birds.

# An Old Horse Knows the Way

| 老 | 马 | 识 | 途 |
|---|---|---|---|
| *lǎo* | *mǎ* | *shí* | *tú* |
| old | horse | to know; knowledge | way, route, road |

**Meaning:** Seniors can put their experience to good use.

This proverb originates from the *Hanfeizi*, a work written by the legalist philosopher Han Feizi at the end of the Warring States period (475–221 BCE). Like his contempories, Han liked to use fables to explain his political philosophy.

## An Old Horse Knows the Way

During the Spring and Autumn period (770–476 BCE), Duke Huan of the state of Qi led his army in an attack against the state of Guzhu. While marching back in triumph, they lost their bearings. They groped in a valley for days but failed to find their way out. Fear began to spread. No one, however, seemed to know the way. They were about to give up when Prime Minister Guan Zhong broke the despairing silence, saying, "I have an idea!"

"Tell us," the anxious duke could not wait.

"We all know that dogs, bees, and pigeons can find their way home. Why can't we put the wisdom of an experienced old horse to the test?" Guan Zhong said, pacing his words, which made everyone even more anxious. "How?" They asked in unison.

The composed Prime Minister continued. "Find an old horse that has been fighting with us on many fronts and let it lead the way!"

Sure enough, by following a veteran horse, Duke Huan and his army eventually came out of the mountains and arrived at the main road leading to the capital. Smiles returned to the faces of the duke and his troops. Stroking and patting the old horse, a soldier exclaimed, "After all, our veteran horse knows the way."

This proverb reminds us to value the experience of people of old age. They have a lot of knowledge and wisdom to share with us.

# 老马识途

这则成语源自《韩非子》，该书作者系战国（公元前475－221年）<u>末期</u>的韩非子。韩非子和他同期的哲学家一样，常常会以讲寓言故事的方式，来<u>阐述</u>他的哲学观点。

　　春秋时期（公元前770－476年），齐桓公带军队攻打了孤竹国，<u>凯旋</u>归来的时候迷了路。他们在一个山谷里转来转去，却始终也找不到回去的路径。大家开始害怕起来，可谁也说不好往哪走。<u>一筹莫展</u>的他们感到莫名的<u>绝望</u>。就在此时，管仲首相突然打破了死一般的沉默，说，"我有主意了。"

　　"快告诉我们，"齐桓公急不可待地说。

　　"我们都知道，狗呀、蜜蜂呀、鸽子呀都能找到家的，我们为什么不能让一匹有经验的老马试一试呢？"管仲<u>不慌不忙</u>地说道。看着他不紧不慢的样子，大家越发着急了。"怎么试呀？"他们<u>异口同声</u>地问。

　　<u>沉着</u>冷静的首相接着说道，"找一匹和我们多年<u>南征北战</u>的老马来，让它走在我们前头。"

　　果不出管仲所料，大家跟随着这匹老马，终于走出大山，来到通往国都的大道上。齐桓公和他的将士们的脸上再次出现了笑容。一个士兵一边<u>抚摸</u>着老马一边说道，"还是老马识途啊。"

## Vocabulary

| Characters | Pinyin | Word Type | Translation |
|---|---|---|---|
| 路途 | lùtú | N. | road, path |
| 末期 | mòqī | N. | end (of a period), final phase |
| 阐述 | chǎnshù | V. | to elaborate on a subject |
| 凯旋 | kǎixúan | V. | to return triumphantly |
| 一筹莫展 | yī chou mò zhǎn | EXPR. | to be at one's wit's end |
| 莫名 | mòmíng | ADJ. | nameless, indescribable |
| 绝望 | juéwàng | N. | despair |
| 不慌不忙 | bù huāng bù máng | EXPR. | unhurried, calm, leisurely |
| 异口同声 | yì kǒu tóng shēng | EXPR. | with one voice, in unison |
| 沉着 | chénzhuó | ADJ. | cool-headed, composed, calm |
| 南征北战 | nán zhēng běi zhàn | EXPR. | war everywhere |
| 抚摸 | fǔmō | V. | to pet |

## Examples

那只老猫被丢在几百公里以外的地方，真是<u>老马识途</u>，最终还是找到了主人的家。

That old cat **really knew its way**. It eventually returned to its owner's home after being abandoned several hundred miles away.

收藏古董，要有<u>老马识途</u>的人指导才行，否则会买到很多赝品。

To collect antiques, one must consult **experienced** collectors. Otherwise one runs the risk of buying a lot of fakes.

# Tricks of a Donkey

| 黔 | 驴 | 之 | 技 |
|---|---|---|---|
| Qián | lú | zhī | jì |
| archaic name for Guizhou Province | donkey, ass | (possessive particle) | skill, trick, ability |

**Literal translation:** The skills of a donkey from Qian.

**Meaning:** Having exhausted one's tactics or skills.

**English equivalent:** Being at one's wit's end.

This proverb comes from the chapter "A Donkey from Qian" of *Three Admonishments*, a collection of fables authored by Liu Zongyuan (773–819 CE), the acclaimed founder of the Classical Prose Movement.

## Tricks of a Donkey

A long time ago, there were no donkeys in the remote place called Qian, a nickname for today's Guizhou Province. A traveling merchant of Qian bought a donkey a few hundred miles away and shipped it back to his hometown. Having no use for the beast, however, the merchant set it free in the wild.

A tiger prowling the wilderness spotted the donkey. The sudden appearance of a strange beast in the territory puzzled the animal king. Deer and hogs were the biggest animals it had ever tackled, but this one was much bigger. The tiger thought that the beast was a supernatural being that had landed there to prey on other animals, including tigers. The fearful thought sent the tiger scampering away, but after a few hundred yards, it stopped. "Why am I running?" The tiger asked itself. "I am the king of the wilderness, and being a king, I should fear nothing. I need to know for sure what that creature is before I show it the respect it deserves." So thinking, the tiger returned to where the donkey was, stalking closer with great caution. Hiding behind a big tree, it discovered that the donkey was doing nothing out of the ordinary. With some confidence, the tiger leapt out from behind the tree and crept over toward the donkey. The strange beast seemed to have heard something stirring, for it stiffened its long ears, blew its white nose, and stomped its black hooves on the ground. Startled, the tiger scurried away, uncertain of what the donkey was up to.

The next day, the tiger went back to the donkey again. It was about to approach the strange creature when, all of a sudden, the donkey brayed, "Heehaw, heehaw, heehaw…" The unfamiliar bellow scared the tiger out of its wits. It only wished that its legs were longer as it dashed into the thick woods.

A few days passed. Curiosity took hold of the tiger once again. It came over to watch the donkey, but saw it grazing peacefully while swiveling its long ears and swishing its tail from time to time. The tiger became bold enough to inch up and tease the donkey, but the donkey responded with the same brays and kicks as before. The tiger jumped back a few yards as if to dodge an imminent attack. Eager to know what else the donkey could do, the tiger decided not to run. Instead, it tried provoking the donkey a second time. Again, the donkey responded with the familiar braying and kicking.

"Ha, ha! That's all the donkey can do!" the tiger chuckled. With this happy realization, it pounced on the donkey and gobbled it up.

This allegorical proverb is comparable to the idiom "at one's wit's end." It has a variant with the same meaning: *qián lǘ jì qióng* 黔驴技穷, whose literal translation is "A donkey of Qian has exhausted its tricks."

# 黔驴之技

这条成语源自柳宗元（公元773－819年）所作的《三戒·黔之驴》。柳宗元被认为是古典散文运动的创始人。

  很久以前，黔，即今日贵州省这个偏远的地方，从来没有过驴这种动物。黔有位<u>行商</u>，从几百里外买回一头驴，托运回老家。然而却发现驴在这个地方没有什么用处，于是就把它放生在野外。

  一只老虎正在野外<u>寻觅</u>食物，看见了驴。在自己的领地里突然出现这么一头<u>诡异</u>的动物，让老虎疑惑<u>不已</u>。平时遇到的体形最大的动物，<u>无非</u>是鹿和野猪之类的。像眼前这么大的动物，还从来没有见过。它以为，这家伙一定是从天而降的天神，<u>下凡</u>来捕食包括虎在内的动物。这么一想，老虎便害怕起来，于是拔腿就逃。但它跑出去没有几百米又停了下来。

  "我跑什么呢？"老虎不禁问自己，"我是百兽之王啊。王是天不怕地不怕的呀。该不该<u>尊重</u>这个家伙，我得先把这家伙搞搞清楚才是。"这么一想，老虎便又回到驴呆的地方。它<u>小心翼翼</u>地靠近驴子，然后隐身在一棵树后，仔细观察驴的<u>动静</u>。看看驴并没有什么特别的动作，胆子便大起来了，于是从树后窜出来，悄悄地向驴子爬过去。驴似乎听到了什么动静，只见它两只长长的耳朵前后转动着，白鼻子<u>喷</u>着粗气，一只前蹄使劲地刨着草地。老虎怕极了，不知驴子要干什么，于是<u>落荒而逃</u>。

  第二天，老虎又回来了，正想接近驴子的时候，驴突然<u>咴儿咴儿</u>地叫了起来。老虎从未听见过这种声音，吓得<u>魂飞魄散</u>，跑进密林里，跑的时候只恨四条腿太短。

  几天过去了。老虎终于<u>按捺</u>不住好奇的心，又回来看一看驴子的动静。看了半天也没有什么异样，只见它正在平静地吃草，耳朵不停地转动着，尾巴不时地甩来甩去。这一回，老虎壮起胆子靠近了驴子，开始逗弄起来。而驴子还是仰起头来咴儿咴儿地叫了几声，<u>撅</u>起后腿<u>尥</u>了几下<u>蹶</u>子。老虎猛地往后一跳，怕驴子发起攻击。为进一步观察驴子，老虎这次没有逃走。他又逗弄起驴子来，而驴子除了<u>司空见惯</u>地又叫又踢以外，也没有什么特别的动作。

"哈哈！原来驴子就会这几招啊！"老虎笑了，知道驴子已经技穷。于是扑上去就把驴子给吃了。

这条寓言成语几乎成了"无计可施"的同义词。该成语派生出一个同义的成语"黔驴技穷"。

## Vocabulary

| Characters | Pinyin | Word Type | Translation |
| --- | --- | --- | --- |
| 行商 | xíngshāng | N. | traveling merchant, peddler |
| 寻觅 | xúnmì | V. | to look for, to seek |
| 诡异 | guǐyì | ADJ. | strange, abnormal |
| 不已 | bùyǐ | ADV. | endlessly, incessantly |
| 无非 | wúfēi | ADV. | nothing but… |
| 下凡 | xiàfán | V. | (gods or immortals) to descent (to the world) |
| 尊重 | zūnzhòng | V. | to respect |
| 小心翼翼 | xiǎoxīn yì yì | ADV. | carefully, cautiously |
| 动静 | dòngjing | N. | movement, activity; the sound of something stirring |
| 平静 | píngjìng | ADJ./ADV. | peaceful/peacefully |
| 落荒而逃 | luòhuāng ér táo | V./EXPR. | to flee (archaic) |
| 喷 | pēn | V. | to spout, spray, sprinkle |
| 咴儿咴儿 | huīrhuīr | ONOM. | whinny, neigh |
| 魂飞魄散 | hún fēi pò sàn | EXPR. | to be scared stiff; lit.: the soul flies away and scatters |
| 按捺 | ànnà | V. | to control, restrain |
| 逗弄 | dòunòng | V. | to tease, provoke |
| 撩 | liāo | V. | to lift up |
| 撂 | liào | V. | to throw or knock down |
| 蹶 | jué | V. | to kick (of a horse or donkey) |
| 司空见惯 | sī kōng jiàn guàn | EXPR. | as usual |
| 招 | zhāo | N. | maneuver, trick |
| 无计可施 | wújìkěshī | EXPR. | at one's wit's end, powerless |

## Examples

我的这点小聪明在父母眼里有如<u>黔驴之技</u>。

In the eyes of my parents, the cleverness I have exhibited actually betrays the fact that I have **exhausted my tricks**.

恐怖份子以人肉炸弹攻击无辜的百姓，无非是<u>黔驴之技</u>，最终逃不过被消灭的下场。

Using human bombs to attack innocent people, the terrorists **are at their wit's end** and ultimately unable to escape the fate of being eliminated.

# Pulling Up Rice Shoots to Help Them Grow

| 揠 | 苗 | 助 | 长 |
|---|---|---|---|
| yà | miáo | zhù | zhǎng |
| to pull up, to eradicate | shoot, sprout, seedling | to help | to grow |

**Meaning:** Spoiling something by being overly enthusiastic or impatient and forcing it ahead.

This proverb comes from a story in part one of the *Gongsun Chou*, by the philosopher Mencius (371–289 BCE), the most famous Confucian after Confucius himself.

## Pulling Up Rice Shoots to Help Them Grow

There was once an impatient farmer in the state of Song. After he transplanted rice seedlings to paddies, he hoped that they would grow into rice overnight. He came to the fields several times a day to watch the seedlings grow. Of course, the more he watched, the less patient he became. One day, he couldn't help jumping into the muddy fields and pulling all the seedlings up an inch. He believed that he was helping them grow faster. When he returned home, his sons were puzzled to see him so exhausted. When asked what he had been doing, he told them that he had been helping the rice shoots grow. "How?" they asked. His response left them speechless. They dashed to the fields, but it was too late: as they had feared, the rice seedlings had already withered.

This proverb teaches us that every process requires a certain amount of time, and trying to rush things won't help. In fact, it can bring disastrous results.

# 揠苗助长

这则成语源自孟子（公元前371-289年）所著的《公孙丑上》。孟子是仅次于孔子的一代儒家宗师。

从前，宋国有个性急的农民。有一年，他把稻秧插进稻田以后，就希望一夜之间长出稻米来。他每天都会来稻田看几次，观察秧苗生长的情况，自然是越看越不耐烦。一天，他终于按捺不住，索性跳进泥泞的稻田里，一颗一颗地把秧苗拔起一寸左右。他认为，这样秧苗会长得更快。回到家，他的儿子们见他精疲力尽，便问他什么原因。他告诉儿子说，他给秧苗催生了。"怎么催生的？"儿子们问道。听到他的回答以后，他的儿子们全都大惊失色。他们二话没说，拔腿就奔到稻田，可是一切都晚了。正像他们所担心的，秧苗早已经枯萎了。

这则成语告诉我们，做事情要循序渐进，急于求成不仅不能成事，有时候反而会造成灾难性的后果。

## Vocabulary

| Characters | Pinyin | Word Type | Translation |
| --- | --- | --- | --- |
| 稻秧 | dàoyāng | N. | rice seedling |
| 插进 | chājìn | V. | to insert, to plug in |
| 稻田 | dàotián | N. | rice paddy |
| 稻米 | dàomǐ | N. | rice (crop) |
| 秧苗 | yāngmiáo | N. | rice seedling |
| 树苗 | shùmiáo | N. | sapling |
| 按捺不住 | àn nà bù zhù | EXPR. | to not be able to hold back |
| 精疲力尽 | jīng pí lì jìn | EXPR. | to be exhausted |
| 催生 | cuīshēng | V. | to help in childbirth |
| 枯萎 | kūwěi | V. | to wither |
| 循序渐进 | xún xù jiàn jìn | EXPR. | step by step |
| 急于 | jíyú | ADJ. | impatient |

## Examples

中国家长逼孩子在课外上很多补习班，这无异于揠苗助长。

Chinese parents force their children to take numerous extracurricular classes. This is like **the farmer who tried to help his rice seedlings grow by pulling them up**.

你一下子给花施这么多肥，小心揠苗助长，把它们毁了。

You're over-fertilizing the flowers. Be careful **not to harm them by improperly hastening their growth**.

# The Dragon Lover Lord Ye

| 叶 | 公 | 好 | 龙 |
|---|---|---|---|
| Yè | gōng | hào | lóng |
| a surname | lord, duke | to like, to be fond of | dragon |

**Literal translation:** Lord Ye likes dragons.

**Meaning:** Professing love for what one actually fears.

This proverb comes from the fifth chapter of *New Prefaces* by Liu Xiang (77–6 BCE), a scholar, author, and government official of the Western Han dynasty. The book records some historical stories and legends, and only ten of its thirty chapters have survived.

## The Dragon Lover Lord Ye

Long ago, a scholar known as Lord Ye (his last name was originally pronounced "She") proclaimed that he loved dragons. Not only did he talk about his fondness for dragons, but he also put his professed affection into practice—and in a big way. He had his clothes embroidered with dragons, his ornaments carved with dragons, and even the sheath of his favorite sword engraved with dragons. Dragon patterns were present everywhere in his house—on the beams, the columns, the walls, the doors, the windows, the curtains, and the beddings. Every piece of his furniture was also a lavish show of dragon art. He read nothing but dragon stories, wrote nothing but dragon tales, and painted nothing but dragon images.

Eventually a heavenly dragon heard of Lord Ye's love for its kind. Very touched, the dragon decided to pay Lord Ye a visit to express its appreciation and make friends with him. One sunny afternoon, Lord Ye was painting dragons in his dragon-adorned studio when, all of a sudden, the sky darkened. Before he realized what had happened, a gigantic dragon stuck its head with bulging eyes and fanged mouth into the window, staring squarely into Lord Ye's terrified eyes. Scared senseless, Lord Ye jumped back and collapsed to the ground unconscious.

This story derides those who pretend to be interested in something that they actually fear or resent.

# 叶公好龙

这个成语源自《新序·杂事五》，作者为刘向（公元前77-6年），是西汉的一位学者、作家和政府官员。该书记录了中国古代历史故事和传说，共三十卷，仅存十章。

很久以前，叶（发音shé）地有个学者，人们管他叫叶公，后来人们逐渐习惯把他的姓读作树叶的叶(yè)了。叶公宣称喜欢龙。他不仅把他的这个喜好昭告天下，而且还付诸实施，搞得动静很大。他衣服上绣着龙，饰物上雕着龙，就连他最心爱的宝剑的剑鞘上也刻着龙。龙的图案在他的寓所无处不在：房梁上、柱子上、墙壁上、门窗上、窗帘上、还有被单上等等。他的每一件家具，都奢华地展现着有关龙的图案。他读书只读有关龙的故事；写作只写有关龙的文字；作画也只描绘龙的身形。

终于有一天，叶公痴情于龙的事儿传到了天龙的耳朵里。天龙十分感动，就想拜访他，跟他交个朋友。一个阳光明媚的下午，叶公正在他到处装潢着龙的图案的书斋里画龙，不知为什么，天一下子昏暗起来。正在他纳闷儿的时候，只见一个龙头蓦地伸进窗来，瞪着双眼，张着满是獠牙的大口。不知所措的叶公正好跟天龙看了个对眼，顿时吓得魂飞魄散，往后踉跄了几步，就昏倒在地不省人事了。

这个故事嘲笑那些假装对一件事感兴趣、实际上却害怕或讨厌这件事的人的虚伪。

## Vocabulary

| Characters | Pinyin | Word Type | Translation |
| --- | --- | --- | --- |
| 传说 | chuánshuō | N. | folktale |
| 宣称 | xuānchēng | V. | to proclaim, to pronounce |
| 昭告 | zhāogào | V. | to declare to the public |
| 付诸实施 | fùzhū shíshī | EXPR. | to carry out, to put into practice |
| 剑鞘 | jiànqiào | N. | the sheath of a sword |
| 无处不在 | wú chù bù zài | EXPR. | to be everywhere |
| 奢华 | shēhuá | ADJ. | luxurious |
| 痴情 | chīqíng | N. | infatuation |
| 感动 | gǎndòng | ADJ. | moved |
| 纳闷 | nàmèn | V. | to be bewildered |
| 蓦 | mò | ADV. | suddenly |
| 伸 | shēn | V. | to stretch |
| 不知所措 | bù zhī suǒ cuò | EXPR. | to be at one's wit's end |
| 魂飞魄散 | hún fēi pò sàn | EXPR. / ADV. | to be scared to death |
| 踉跄 | liàngqiàng | V. | to stumble, to stagger |
| 昏倒 | hūndǎo | V. | to faint |
| 不省人事 | bù xǐng rén shì | EXPR. | to lose consciousness |
| 虚伪 | xūwěi | ADJ. / N. | hypocritical, hypocrisy |

## Examples

他跟谁都说他喜欢蜥蜴，可有一天，我拿了一只给他看，他却不敢正视，真是<u>叶公好龙</u>。

He tells everyone that he likes lizards, but he didn't even have the guts to take a real look at the one I brought to show him the other day. **He's like Lord Ye, who only professed his love for dragons but feared them in reality.**

很多人像<u>叶公好龙</u>一样，嘴上喊着改革；可是，真要是改革了，他们又受不了了。

A lot of people are like **Lord Ye, who pretended to love dragons but actually feared them**, for they pay lip service to reform, but when it really happens, they're unable to take it.

# The Fool Set on Moving a Mountain

| 愚 | 公 | 移 | 山 |
|---|---|---|---|
| yú | gōng | yí | shān |
| to be foolish | gentleman, lord | to (re)move | mountain |

**Literal translation:** A foolish old man moves a mountain.

**Meaning:** Persevering in the face of seemingly insurmountable difficulties.

This proverb first appeared in the chapter "The Questions of Tang" in the *Liezi*, a Daoist text allegedly written by Lie Yukou, a fifth century BCE philosopher whose authenticity is still unconfirmed. Some scholars argue that Lie Yukou was a character fabricated by Zhuangzi, a philosopher who lived in the fourth century BCE. In 1945, Mao Zedong, chairman of the Communist Party of China, quoted the story behind the proverb in his closing remarks at the Party's Seventh Congress in Yan'an.

## The Fool Set on Moving a Mountain

A long time ago, to the south of Jizhou and the north of Heyang, somewhere on the Great Plains of China, there stood two big mountains, one called Taihang, and the other Wangwu. They were both thousands of feet high and together covered an area of seven hundred miles.

At the foot of the mountains on the northern side, there lived a family headed by an old man in his nineties. Still robust and healthy, he went to work in the fields with his sons and grandsons every day. People didn't know his real name but simply called him Yugong, or Mr. Foolish. They thought him foolish because they mistook his perseverance for stubbornness. Mr. Foolish and his family found it hard to make a living because of the Taihang and Wangwu mountains as their farmland was on the other side. Every day, they had to spend a great deal of time traveling back and forth.

One evening, Mr. Foolish called his family together. "How about removing the mountains from our house?" he asked. Before anyone had time to answer, he continued, "If we don't give up, we can open up a road that leads directly to our farmland on the Han River. What do you think?" His question took none by surprise, for they knew him only too well. Besides, they desired to have easy access to their farmland as much as he did. Seeing that the patriarch had already made up his mind, they all showed their support. His wife, however, had some doubt.

"You're too old to even flatten a mound. How can you get rid of these mountains?" she asked. "Besides, where should we dump the rocks and dirt we dig up?"

"We can throw them into the Bohai Sea," suggested their youngest son, who stood up rolling up his sleeves in excitement.

The next day, the entire family turned out carrying picks, chisels, shovels, and baskets. Even some of the neighbors, including a seven-year-old boy, joined them. They dug and dug, and chiseled and chiseled, and they took the rocks and dirt to the Bohai Sea. As it was hundreds of miles away, it took them an entire year to make a round trip.

Meanwhile, in the upper reaches of the Han River on the other side of the mountains, there lived a Mr. Smart. He gave himself the nickname because he was quite smug about his intelligence, claiming that he had never done anything stupid. Curious about what was happening on the other side of the mountains, Mr. Smart came over to find out for himself.

When he learned of Mr. Foolish's ambitious plan, he chuckled with amusement. "What can I say? You are truly worthy of the name Mr. Foolish! Don't you know how old you are? Do you think you can chisel away even a fraction of the mountains in your lifetime?" he chided.

"Well, I don't think you're really that smart," Mr. Foolish retorted. "You have no idea that my sons will continue working after I die. When they pass away, their sons will do the same. And they will have their sons and grandsons so that the family line will never end. The mountains, however, will never grow. An inch chiseled away is an inch less. What do you say?" Mr. Smart was speechless.

A local God of Soil and Ground reported what Mr. Foolish said and did to his divine superior, the Jade Emperor of Heaven. Touched by the dauntless spirit of Mr. Foolish and his family, the celestial emperor sent two of his giants to help them. The giants plucked up Mt. Taihang and placed it miles away on the east side of Mr. Foolish's house. Then they pulled up Mt. Wangwu and carried it somewhere an equal distance to the south. As a result, the family now could enjoy a full view of their farmland from the back windows of their house.

This proverb teaches us that difficulties can be overcome eventually through our perseverance.

# 愚公移山

这条成语最早出现在道学典籍《列子·汤问》中，该书据说由公元前5世纪的列御寇编撰。然而，作者真伪仍然是个谜，有学者干脆认为列御寇是庄子杜撰出来的。中国共产党主席毛泽东于1945年在延安召开的七中全会闭幕式上发言时，<u>引用</u>了《愚公移山》的典故。其发言在文化大革命（1966–1976）早期，与毛的另外两篇文章以《老三篇》的题目集成小册子发表，从而使这个成语<u>家喻户晓</u>。

很久以前，在华北的冀州之南，河阳之北，耸立着两座大山，一座叫太行，一座叫王屋。山高均为千<u>尺</u>，共占地方圆七百里。

北边山脚下住着一户人家，家长年逾九十，身体却依然<u>硬朗</u>，每天照常和儿孙们一起下地干活。由于不知其真实姓名，人们<u>索性</u>管他叫愚公，这是因为人们把他<u>坚韧不拔</u>错看作是<u>冥顽不灵</u>了。大山挡在房前，把这家人与他们劳作的田地隔开，给他们的生活带来极大的不便，光是每天往返都要花费很长时间。

一天晚上，愚公把全家人召集到一起。他开门见山地问大家："把山从咱家门口移开怎么样？"还没等人们开口，愚公就说了下去，"如果我们坚持下去，我们就能开出一条直通咱家田地的路。你们说呢？"家人对愚公的<u>秉性</u>十分了解，对他的想法一点儿也没感到突然。<u>再说</u>他们也想方方便便地去种田。既然<u>老人家</u>主意已定，他们便毫不犹豫地表示了<u>支持</u>。然而，愚公的<u>老伴儿</u>却质疑道："你这么大年纪<u>铲平</u>个土包都费力，要搬掉两座山<u>吃得消</u>吗？还有，挖下的土石放在哪儿？"愚公的小儿子，一边撸着袖子站起来，一边激动地说："咱们把土石倒渤海里去"。

第二天，愚公一家全都出动了，有的拿着<u>镐</u>，有的握着<u>凿</u>，有的扛着<u>锹</u>，还有的端着<u>簸箕</u>。一些邻居也赶来帮忙，其中有个男孩儿才七岁。他们挖的挖、凿的凿，一次次把挖凿出的土石运往渤海去<u>倾倒</u>。由于距渤海数百<u>里</u>，一个来回要花掉他们一年的工夫。

汉河上游太行和王屋山的另一面，住着老头儿，自诩"智叟"，因为觉得自己很聪明，从不做傻事。山这边的动静引起了他的好奇，他于是过来想看个究竟。当他听愚公说要挖掉两座山的时候，觉得十分可笑。"嘿嘿，让我怎么说你呢？叫你愚公一点儿都不<u>冤</u>！你不知道你多大年纪了么？你觉得这一辈子能把山凿下一个角来吗？"智叟<u>揶揄</u>道。

"依我看,你这'智叟'算是白叫了,"愚公反唇相讥道:"你怎么会想到,我走了,我儿子会继续干下去;等我儿子没了,他们的儿子也会干下去。他们的儿子会有他们儿子和孙子,这样子子孙孙,无穷无尽。而山却不会加高,铲掉一寸是一寸。你说呢?"听完这话,智叟无言以对。

当地的土地爷把愚公移山的事迹,报告给了天上的玉皇大帝。玉皇大帝也为愚公坚韧不拔的精神所感动,遂派两个巨人下凡来帮助愚公一家解困。巨人先把太行山拔起来,放置在愚公家数里外的东面;然后又把王屋山提起来,安放在愚公家数里外的南面。自此,愚公一家从后窗就能看到自家的田地了。

这条成语告诉人们,只要坚持不屑地努力,困难最终会被克服。

## Vocabulary

| Characters | Pinyin | Word Type | Translation |
| --- | --- | --- | --- |
| 引用 | yǐnyòng | V. | to quote from, to cite |
| 家喻户晓 | jiā yù hù xiǎo | EXPR. | known to everyone |
| 尺 | chǐ | MEASURE | 1 *chi* = 1.09 ft. |
| 硬朗 | yìnglǎng | ADJ. | healthy, strong |
| 索性 | suǒxìng | ADV. | simply, just |
| 坚韧不拔 | jiānrèn bù bá | ADJ., ADV. | persistent; persistently |
| 冥顽不灵 | míng wán bù líng | ADJ./EXPR. | stubborn, stupid |
| 秉性 | bǐngxìng | N. | inborn character, personality |
| 支持 | zhīchí | V./N. | to support, to be in favor of; agreement |
| 老伴儿 | lǎobànr | N. | (colloq.) spouse of an elderly person |
| 铲平 | chǎnpíng | V. | to flatten, to level |
| 吃得消 | chīdexiāo | EXPR. | to be able to, to endure |
| 镐 | gǎo | N./V. | pick; to pick |
| 凿 | záo | N./V. | chisel; to chisel |
| 锹 | xiān | N. | shovel |
| 簸箕 | bòji | N. | bamboo or wicker basket |
| 冤 | yuān | N./ADJ. | injustice; wrong |
| 揶揄 | yēyú | V. | to ridicule, deride, tease |
| 反唇相讥 | fǎn chún xiāng jī | EXPR./V. | to retort, answer back sarcastically |
| 无言以对 | wú yán yǐ duì | EXPR./ADJ. | speechless |
| 土地爷 | Tǔdìyé | PN. | God of Soil and Ground (Chinese myth.) |
| 玉皇大帝 | Yùhuáng dàdì | PN. | Jade Emperor of Heaven (Chinese myth.) |
| 放置 | fàngzhì | V. | to place, to set |
| 安放 | ānfàng | V. | to place, to set |

## Examples

中国人凭着愚公移山的精神，建成了世界上里程最远的高铁系统。

With their **perseverance and diligence**, the Chinese have built the longest mileage of high-speed rails in the world.

他发扬愚公移山的精神，用了十年的功夫，编纂了这部词典。

In the spirit of **an old man trying to remove a mountain**, as told in a Chinese myth, he has devoted a decade of his lifetime to compiling this dictionary.

# A Man from Zheng Shops for Shoes

| 郑 | 人 | 买 | 履 |
|---|---|---|---|
| Zhèng | rén | mǎi | lǚ |
| a state during the Warring States Period | person | to buy | shoe (archaic; modern Chinese 鞋 xié) |

郑人买履

**Meaning:** To bind yourself by old, nonfunctional, or limiting structures, rules, or practices.

This proverb comes from the "Outer Congeries of Sayings, the Upper Left Series" in the *Hanfeizi*, a text by Han Feizi (c. 280–233 BCE), a famous philosopher, essayist, and political commentator, as well as one of the leading Legalists of the pre-Qin era.

## A Man from Zheng Shops for Shoes

Once upon a time, a man from the state of Zheng wanted to buy a pair of new shoes. He measured his foot with twine, marked off the size, and cut off the length of twine to have as a measurement of his foot size. In his rush, however, he left the twine at home when he headed out to the market.

At the market, he came to a shoe stall and, after a lot of picking and choosing, finally decided on a pair of shoes that he liked. Wondering if the shoes would fit his feet, he thought of his twine and dug all through his gown for it, but in vain. Just as the shoe seller was looking really puzzled, the man slapped his forehead and blurted out to himself, "Stupid me! I left the twine at home." Turning to the shoe seller, he said, "Keep the shoes for me. I'm going home to get my measurement." Then he rushed away, leaving the shoe seller baffled.

He arrived at home panting heavily and, after retrieving the piece of twine, hurried back to the market. Unfortunately, it had closed.

Later, when his neighbors learned of his absurdity, they asked, "Why did you waste your time going back and forth from your home to the market? Why didn't you try the shoes on with your feet right at the shoe stall?" The man of Zheng replied, "I'd rather trust my measurement than my feet."

This proverb satirizes those who stubbornly cling to old conventions without regard for realities that call for flexibility.

# 郑人买履

这条成语出自《韩非子·外储说左上》。《韩非子》的作者韩非是中国先秦时期著名的哲学家、思想家、政论家和散文家，也是法家的代表人物之一。

从前，郑国有个人，打算到<u>集市</u>上买双新鞋穿。他先用绳子量了脚，把多余的部分剪去以后作为<u>尺码</u>。可是临走时<u>粗心大意</u>，竟把尺码忘在家里刚才坐过的地方。

他来到集市一家卖鞋的摊位前。好不容易挑选好一双中意的鞋子，想拿出尺码来量一量鞋子，看看是否和自己的脚相<u>匹配</u>。可是<u>翻遍</u>全身，也找不到做尺码的绳子。卖鞋人正在<u>纳闷</u>的时候，只见他脑门一拍，<u>自言自语</u>地说，"瞧我这<u>记性</u>，把尺码忘在家里了！"于是就对卖鞋的人说："鞋子先给我放好，等我回家把尺码拿来再买。"说完，就急匆匆地跑回家了，弄得卖鞋人丈二<u>和尚摸不着头脑</u>。

他气喘吁吁地奔回家，拿了尺码，又<u>慌慌张张</u>地赶回集市。可惜，这时集市早已经散了。

后来，<u>街坊们</u>知道了这件事，觉得很奇怪，就问他："你为什么不用自己的脚当场试一试鞋子，而偏偏要回家去取尺码，白白地浪费了时间呢？"这个买鞋的郑国人却说："我宁愿相信量好的尺码，也不相信我的脚。"

这条成语讽刺那些不顾客观实际而<u>墨守成规</u>的人。

## Vocabulary

| Characters | Pinyin | Word Type | Translation |
|---|---|---|---|
| 集市 | jíshì | N. | market, country fair |
| 尺码 | chǐmǎ | N. | measurement, size, fitting |
| 粗心大意 | cūxīn dàyì | ADJ. | careless |
| 匹配 | pǐpèi | V. | to match up with something |
| 翻遍 | fānbiàn | V. | to ransack, to turn everything over |
| 纳闷 | nà mèn | ADJ. | confused, puzzled |
| 自言自语 | zì yán zì yǔ | V. | to talk to oneself |
| 丈二和尚摸不着头脑 | zhàng èr héshàng mōbùzháo tóunǎo | EXPR./ADJ. | lit. can't touch the head of the ten-foot monk; fig. confused, puzzled, can't make heads or tails of something |
| 慌慌张张 | huānghuāng zhāngzhāng | EXPR./ADV. | helter-skelter |
| 墨守成规 | mò shǒu chéng guī | EXPR./ADJ. | be bound by convention |

## Examples

我们做事要根据实际的情况进行灵活调整，千万不能像郑人买履一样。

When we do something, we need to make adjustments as needed instead of **adamantly sticking to a counterproductive plan**.

有人说，现在的企业招聘，对应聘者只按规定的要求取舍，丝毫也不考虑他们的实际能力，这种做法和郑人买履差不多。

Some believe that employers today are like **the man who used a measurement of his feet rather than his feet themselves to see if some new shoes would fit**: they hire people according to rigid written requirements without regard for candidates' actual abilities.

# Your Own Spear Against Your Own Shield

| 自 | 相 | 矛 | 盾 |
|---|---|---|---|
| zì | xiāng | máo | dùn |
| oneself, one's own | mutual, each other | spear | shield |

**Literal translation:** Mutual spear and shield.

**Meaning:** Contradicting oneself.

This proverb is derived from the chapter "Criticisms of the Ancients, Series One" in the *Hanfeizi*, a book compiled by a Legalist philosopher of the same name during the Warring States Period (475–221 BCE).

## Your Own Spear Against Your Own Shield

In the state of Chu, a weapon-monger was hawking a spear and a shield in a market. Brandishing the spear, he called out, "Everybody! Take a close look at this spear. It's made of a special metal. Sharp as can be. I am not bragging. It's so sharp it can penetrate any shield—metal, rattan, or leather!"

People in the market began to gather around, curious to see the invincible spear. Encouraged by his self-perceived marketing talent, the seller began to advertise his shield in the same fashion. He held it above his head and hollered, "Look at this shield! It's made of the best leather in the world. It's so tough that nothing can penetrate it!"

The man was feeling immensely proud of himself when someone in the crowd called out, "Hey, you just said you had a spear that could pierce anything in the world, and now you're telling us that this shield could resist anything sharp. How about trying your spear on your shield and see what happens!" The crowd bellowed, echoing his demand. The weapon-monger was speechless. Blushing with shame, he withdrew dejectedly from the jeering crowd, dragging his spear and shield.

This proverb is used to criticize one who contradicts oneself in speech or action. Incidentally, the characters for spear (矛 *máo*) and shield (盾 *dùn*) in this proverb gave birth to the compound Chinese word 矛盾 *máodùn*, which means a contradiction.

# 自相矛盾

这条成语出自《韩非子·难一》。《韩非子》一书由同名作者、战国时期的法家哲学大师韩非子所作。

楚国有个卖兵器的，在集市上叫卖矛和盾。他一边挥舞着手中的长矛，一边吆喝着："嘿，都来瞧，都来看啦！我这支长矛，是特种合金打造的，锋利无比。我不是吹牛，这么跟你们说吧，不管你的盾是用金属、白藤还是皮革做的，我这矛一扎可就透啊！"

集市上的人们开始聚拢过来，想看看这支天下无敌的长矛究竟是个什么样子。卖兵器的人开始为自己的营售禀赋飘飘然起来，于是又用同样的方法，推销起他的盾来。他一边把盾牌举过头顶，一边吆喝着，"诸位看好了，这只盾可是用天下最好的皮革打造的，坚固得不得了，无论多么尖锐的武器都刺不穿啊。"

正当卖兵器的人洋洋自得的时候，忽然人群里有人喊了起来："喂，你刚才还在说，你的矛能穿透世上任何坚固的东西，怎么这会儿你的盾又刀枪不入了呢？干脆，用你的矛刺一刺你的盾给我们看看怎么样啊？"人群开始沸腾起来，纷纷要他拿自己的矛试一试自己的盾，弄得卖兵器的人一句话也说不出来。他只好拖着矛和盾，面红耳赤地离开了集市，离开了一阵阵的嘲笑声。

这条成语是用来批评那些说话或做事前后不一的人。而其中的"矛"和"盾"两个字后来合成了"矛盾"这个词。

## Vocabulary

| Characters | Pinyin | Word Type | Translation |
| --- | --- | --- | --- |
| 哲学 | zhéxué | N. | philosophy |
| 兵器 | bīngqì | N. | weapon, especially pre-firearm |
| 吆喝 | yāohé | V. | to yell, to shout, to hawk |
| 藤 | téng | N. | rattan, vine |
| 锋利 | fēnglì | ADJ. | sharp (especially used to describe weapons such as knives and swords) |
| 吹牛 | chuīniú | V. | to brag |
| 扎透 | zhátòu | V. | to penetrate |
| 天赋 | tiānfù | N. | gift, natural talent |
| 天下无敌 | tiān xià wú dí | ADJ. | matchless, without equal (literal meaning: no match under heaven) |
| 洋洋自得 | yáng yáng zì dé | ADJ. | very self-satisfied |
| 沸腾 | fèiténg | V. | to boil, to flare up |
| 面红耳赤 | miàn hóng ěr chì | EXPR. | lit. face red and ears scarlet, flushed with anger or excitement |

## Examples

你一会儿说爱我，一会儿又说讨厌我，你这不是<u>自相矛盾</u>吗？

One minute you say you love me. Another minute you say you dislike me. Aren't you **contradicting yourself**?

你说你主张和平，可今天你却给这个开战的提案投了赞成票。这是<u>自相矛盾</u>！

You said you wanted peace, but today you voted for this resolution to start the war. You're **being self-contradictory**!

# Intermediate Proverbs

# Dong Shi Mimics a Frown

| 东施 | 效 | 颦 |
|---|---|---|
| Dōng Shī | xiào | pín |
| Dong Shi | to imitate | to scowl, to knit the brow |

**Literal translation:** Dong Shi mimics knitting her brow.

**Meaning:** Making a fool of oneself by mimicking what somebody else is doing; being a copycat.

This proverb comes from the section "The Turning of Heaven" in the *Zhuangzi,* a book attributed to Zhuangzi (c. 369–286 BCE, also known as Zhuang Zhou ), who was a celebrated Daoist philosopher and a man of letters during the Warring States period.

## Dong Shi Mimics a Frown

According to legend, there was a beautiful young woman named Xi Shi who lived in the state of Yue during the Spring and Autumn period (770–476 BCE). She was known not only for her gorgeous looks but also for her graceful moves. The young women in her village often imitated her dress and makeup, and they even copied her bearing unwittingly from time to time. No matter how she carried herself, Xi Shi was pleasing to their eyes. For a time, Xi Shi suffered from heartburn, and whenever it hit, she would frown and press her hand to her chest. Even this sickly posture made her all the more attractive to her fellow villagers.

In Xi Shi's neighborhood there lived another young woman of her age. Dong Shi by name, she was homely and envied Xi Shi for her beauty. She closely studied Xi Shi's each and every move, including the expressions and movements induced by her illness. Dong Shi began to mimic her, knitting her brows and clutching her chest like Xi Shi. However, by doing so, the already ugly Dong Shi made herself appear all the more unsightly. Men and women alike shunned the sight of her. Feeling embarrassed and wronged at the same time, Dong Shi could not figure out why people treated her and Xi Shi so differently even though they were acting the same way. How could she know that beauty is intrinsic and therefore could not be copied?

This proverb is a burlesque of those who mimic others only to make a laughing stock of themselves. Chinese people also like to use the proverb as an expression of modesty when talking about themselves trying to learn something from others.

# 东施效颦

这条成语出自《庄子·天运》，作者庄周（约前369年－前286年），战国中期人，是中国历史上著名的思想家、哲学家和文学家。

相传春秋时候，越国有个名叫西施的姑娘，不仅有<u>沉鱼落雁</u>之容，<u>闭月羞花</u>之貌，而且就是平时所做的任何一个动作，都是楚楚动人。因此，村里常有一些姑娘模仿她的衣着打扮；偶尔还有些姑娘有意无意地模仿她的姿态。无论西施怎样，大家看着都顺眼。有一段时间，西施患了胃病，泛酸难受的时候，总爱捂着胸口、紧皱着眉头。即使这样一个病态，也让人们觉得<u>妩媚</u>可爱。

西施有个邻居名叫东施，和她一样年轻，但样貌很一般。她十分羡慕西施，常常留意西施的一举一动。西施捂胸皱眉的样子，她也跟着学了起来。本来长得就不好看，现在让人看了更加<u>丑陋不堪</u>。无论男女，谁见了都不愿意瞧她一眼。这番情景让东施感觉又<u>尴尬</u>又<u>委屈</u>，她怎么也想不通，同是一个动作，为什么西施做了人们喜欢，而自己做了却招致人们的<u>厌恶</u>呢？她哪里知道，西施的美完全出于她的<u>天生丽质</u>，只靠假装和模仿怎么能做得到呢？

这条成语比喻模仿别人，不但模仿不好，反而<u>出丑</u>。有时也作<u>自谦</u>之词，表示自己根底差，学别人的长处没有学到家。

## Vocabulary

| Characters | Pinyin | Word Type | Translation |
|---|---|---|---|
| 沉鱼落雁 | chén yú luò yàn | EXPR. | lit. fish sink, goose alight (also from the *Zhuangzi*); used to describe the extreme beauty of a woman |
| 闭月羞花 | bì yuè xiū huā | EXPR. | lit. hiding the moon, shaming the flower; used to describe the extreme beauty of a women |
| 妩媚 | wǔmèi | ADJ. | charming |
| 丑陋 | chǒulòu | ADJ. | ugly |
| 不堪 | bùkān | V./ADJ. | to be unable to bear; extremely |
| 尴尬 | gāngà | ADJ. | embarrassed, awkward-feeling |
| 委屈 | wěiqu | ADJ./N. | to feel wronged; grievance |
| 厌恶 | yànwù | V. | to loathe; to be disgusted with something |
| 天生丽质 | tiānshēng lìzhì | N. | natural beauty |
| 出丑 | chūchǒu | V. | to make a fool of oneself |
| 自谦 | zìqiān | ADJ. | modest |

## Examples

她的歌喉并不好，偏喜欢模仿一个著名的歌星唱歌，真是<u>东施效颦</u>，自暴其短。

She lacks a good voice and **prefers to imitate** a famous singer. The more she does so, however, the more of her own weaknesses she exposes.

甲：啊，你的舞蹈跳得太棒了！

乙：大家过奖了，这个舞是大舞蹈家杨丽萍经常跳的，我不过是<u>东施效颦</u>罢了。

A: Wow, your dance was awesome!

B: Thanks! I feel flattered. This dance is performed often by the famous dancer Yang Liping. **I am only imitating her.**

# Learning to Walk in Handan

| 邯郸 | 学 | 步 |
|---|---|---|
| *Hándān* | *xué* | *bù* |
| Handan (capital city) | to learn | step |

**Literal translation:** Handan learns to walk.

**Alternate translation:** A man from Handan learns to walk.

**Meaning:** By slavishly imitating others, one can lose one's own individuality and creativity.

This proverb stems from the *Zhuangzi*, a collection of Daoist philosophy allegedly compiled by the namesake of the book, the Daoist philosopher Zhuangzi (c. 369–286 BCE, also known as Zhuang Zhou). He was a follower of Laozi, the founder of Daoism. Philosophically, *dao* means the Way (of the universe). While Laozi believed that the Way could only be understood without verbal explanation, Zhuangzi tried to explain it with allegories, including the one below.

## Learning to Walk in Handan

The allegory originated in an encounter between a man named Gongsun Long and a prince named Wei Mou. Gongsun Long thought of himself as the most learned man in the world until he met Zhuangzi, whose philosophy he found too hard to understand. He went to Wei Mou, a prince of Wei State, for help. Thinking that Gongsun Long's vision was too limited to comprehend Zhuangzi, Wei Mou tried to dissuade him from obsessing over Zhuangzi's theories and urged him to be himself. To make his point, he told Gongsun Long an allegory, which Zhuangzi later repeated, about a young man learning how to walk in Handan.

The young man was from Shouling in the state of Yan. While out walking one day, he heard that people from the neighboring Zhao state all walked in a particularly elegant manner. Despite his family's disapproval, the young man made up his mind to visit Handan, capital of Zhao, to learn their gait even though his posture of walking was fine. In Handan, he followed anyone who came into sight, be it man or woman, young or old. He imitated the way they walked, but within half a month, he found himself in an awkward situation: not only had he failed to learn the Handan walk, but he had also forgotten his own original bearing. He had to crawl all the way back home to Shouling, making himself a laughing stock before onlookers, his villagers, and even his own family members.

This proverb teaches us not to be so intent on imitating others that we forget our own uniqueness, strengths, and skills.

# 邯郸学步

这则成语，源自一部<u>阐述</u>道教思想的论著《<u>庄子</u>》。该书作者据说是公元前四世纪的中国哲学家庄周，也叫庄子，与其书同名。庄子是道教创始人老子的<u>忠实</u>信徒。从哲学意义上讲，所谓"道"，既是宇宙万物之规律。老子认为"道"只能<u>意会</u>不能言传；而庄子却常以<u>寓言</u>的方式，对其加以<u>阐释</u>。以下寓言即是一例。

公孙龙原以为自己是世界上最有学问的人，有一天遇到了庄子，却发现他的哲学思想深奥得听不懂。公孙龙于是求教于魏国的公子魏牟。魏牟深知，公孙龙眼界<u>狭窄</u>，是无法理解庄子的，<u>遂</u>劝他做好自己就行了，不要再为无法达到庄子的高度而<u>纠结</u>。他还给公孙龙讲了两个"邯郸学步"的寓言故事，来说明自己的观点。便是其中之一。

燕国寿陵有个少年，一天，走在街上，听到人们在<u>交头接耳</u>地议论着邻国赵国的百姓，说他们走起路来，个个都十分优雅。这位寿陵少年一听，便<u>不顾</u>家庭反对，<u>执意</u>要到赵国的国都邯郸去看个<u>究竟</u>。尽管他自己走路完全没有问题，他还是要学邯郸人的步态。在邯郸城里，他不分男女老幼，见谁学谁，<u>一丝不苟</u>地模仿人家走路的样子。不出半个月，这个寿陵少年，不仅没有学会邯郸人走路的优雅，反而把自己原来走路的<u>姿势</u>也给忘了，不得不趴着回到燕国寿陵的家。他的行为，不光招致路人和村民的耻笑，也让家人把他当作笑柄。

这则成语告诉我们，不要只想着去模仿别人，结果把自己特点、优势和技等都给忘记了。

## Vocabulary

| Characters | Pinyin | Word Type | Translation |
| --- | --- | --- | --- |
| 邯郸 | *Hándān* | PN. | Handan, capital of Zhao (a city in modern-day Hebei Province) |
| 阐述; 阐释 | *chǎnshù; chǎnshì* | V. | to elaborate, to treat (a topic); to explain |
| 忠实 | *zhōngshí* | ADJ. | faithful, loyal |
| 意会 | *yìhuì* | V. | to sense, to grasp intuitively |
| 寓言 | *yùyán* | N. | fable, story |
| 狭窄 | *xiázhǎi* | ADJ. | narrow |
| 遂 | *suì* | ADV. | then, thereupon |
| 纠结 | *jiūjié* | V. | to be linked, to intertwine |
| 交头接耳 | *jiāo tóu jiē ěr* | EXPR. | to whisper in each other's ear |
| 不顾 | *bùgù* | PREP./V. | despite, in spite of, although; to ignore |
| 执意 | *zhíyì* | V. | to insist on, to be determined |
| 究竟 | *jiūjìng* | V. | get to the bottom of something, find out |
| 一丝不苟 | *yī sī bù gǒu* | EXPR. | lit. not one thread loose; fig. meticulous, following exactly by the rules |
| 姿势 | *zīshì* | N. | posture, position |

## Examples

有些大陆文艺主持人，盲目学习港台腔，结果是<u>邯郸学步</u>，不但港台腔说得不纯，就连普通话也不会说了。

Some hosts of entertainment TV programs in China blindly imitate the accents of TV hosts from Hong Kong and Taiwan. In the end, they not only fail to learn the proper Hong Kong or Taiwanese accent, but they also forget their original Mandarin style.

他本来国画画得挺不错的，却非要改学油画。结果是<u>邯郸学步</u>，不但油画没学会，国画也画得不伦不类了。

He was pretty good at traditional Chinese painting, but he insisted on forsaking that style in favor of oil techniques. The result was miserable: not only did he fail to learn oil painting, but he was also no longer able to create authentic Chinese paintings.

# Monkeys Rescuing the Moon

| 猴子 | 救 | 月 |
|---|---|---|
| hóuzǐ | jiù | yuè |
| monkey | to save, rescue | moon |

**Meaning:** Worrying over nothing.

This proverb comes from the *Forest of Gems in the Garden of the Dharma* written by Dao Shi in 668 CE. This 100-volume work containing Buddhist and other ancient texts is considered an encyclopedia of Buddhism.

猴子救月

## Monkeys Rescuing the Moon

A long time ago, outside of Varanasi (Benares), the capital of the Kingdom of Kashi, there was a big forest seldom visited by humans. It was home to a few hundred monkeys. One night, the monkeys came out to play and wandered to a well. They were having fun frolicking when suddenly a young monkey screamed with fear, "Oh no! The moon is fallen into the well!"

An elderly monkey rushed over, looked down into the well, and saw the moon floating on the surface of the water. Alarmed as well, he said to his fellow monkeys, "Indeed, the moon has dropped into the well. We must work together to fish it out; otherwise, the whole world will be pitch black every night."

"But how can we?" asked a monkey. The entire troop hushed.

"I got it!" The elderly monkey blurted out after a moment, breaking the silence. "We're lucky! See this tree here and its branches extending over the well? I'll climb up and hold on to one of the branches. Then one of you come up and hold on to my tail, and another hold on to the tail of the one that holds mine. This way, we'll be able to form a chain to reach the moon in the well."

Hearing this, all the monkeys sighed with relief. Immediately, the strongest young adults volunteered and formed a chain as the elderly monkey had instructed them. The monkey at the end of the chain locked its feet tightly with the tail of its fellow monkey above and reached its hands into the water, working hard to fish the moon out. Each time its hands touched the water, however, the moon would break into pieces. The monkey would wait till the moon came together again before making another attempt.

He went on like this while the troop of monkeys around the well cheered in support. The trouble was that each of the monkey's movements gave the chain of monkeys a jerk. It then swung and swayed until the branch that the elderly monkey was grasping snapped. All the monkeys splashed into the well. As the bedraggled monkeys managed to clamber out with the help of the onlookers, one of them happened to raise its head. Not believing in what it saw, the monkey shrieked, "Look! The moon's still up there!"

This proverb warns people against making trouble out of nothing, lest they get hurt by their groundless worries. A derivative two-part version, "Monkeys fishing for the moon—all for naught" (*hóu zǐ lāo yuè, yì chǎng kōng* 猴子捞月，一场空), means "an effort that proves fruitless."

# 猴子救月

这条成语出自《法苑珠林·愚赣篇·杂痴部》。由道世完成于668的这部百卷巨著，被认为是佛学的百科全书。

从前有一个伽师国，首都是波罗奈城。在城郊人迹罕至的森林中，生存着数百只猴子。一天晚上，这群猴子嬉戏着来到了一口井旁。不知是哪只猴子惊恐地喊叫起来："不好了，月亮掉到井里去了！"

一只年长的猴子一听，赶过来看了看井中的月亮，便对同伴们说："月亮真的掉到井里了。我们应该一起努力把它捞上来，免得叫世界上每个夜晚都黑漆漆的。"

"可怎么才能把月亮捞出来呢？"猴群中有一只问道。随即猴群变得鸦雀无声。

那只年长的猴子一拍脑壳："有办法了，我攀在树枝上，你们其中一个拽住我的尾巴，一个连一个，就可以把月亮捞出来了。"

猴子们听罢全都长舒了一口气。那些最强壮的年轻猴子自告奋勇，按照老猴的吩咐，一个接一个，连成了一长串。最后一只猴子把两脚紧紧地抓住上边那个同伴的尾巴，把腾出的前爪伸进水里去捞月亮。可是，它刚一触摸到水面，月亮就碎了。这只猴子便等着月亮复原，再伸手去捞。

捞啊捞，每捞一次，猴子组成的长串就要跟着晃动一下。就这样晃来晃去，老猴儿攀着的树枝终于不堪重负，"咔嚓"一声折断了，长串上的猴子全都掉进了水里。井边助阵的同伴把他们捞了上来，等浑身湿漉漉的猴子们爬出井口时，有只猴子偶然抬起头来，不禁大惊失色："看啊！月亮还在天上挂着哪！"

这则成语常被用来告诫人们，没事找事会让自己受到伤害。该成语派生出"猴子捞月，一场空"这个歇后语，意思不言自明。

## Vocabulary

| Characters | Pinyin | Word Type | Translation |
| --- | --- | --- | --- |
| 人迹罕至 | rén jì hǎn zhì | EXPR. | lit. where human footprints are rare; fig. deserted, uninhabited |
| 嬉戏 | xīxì | V. | to frolic, to play |
| 惊恐 | jīngkǒng | ADJ. | terrified; horrified |
| 黑漆漆 | hēi qīqī | ADJ. | pitch dark |
| 捞 | lāo | V. | to fish something from water |
| 随即 | suíjí | ADV. | immediately, at once |
| 鸦雀无声 | yāquè wú shēng | EXPR. | deadly silent |
| 脑壳 | nǎoké | N. | skull, brain |
| 拽 | zhuài | V. | to drag; to hold on to something |
| 自告奋勇 | zìgào fènyǒng | EXPR. | to volunteer |
| 吩咐 | fēnfù | V./N. | to command, instruct; command |
| 晃动 | huàngdòng | V. | to swing |
| 不堪重负 | bù kān zhòng fù | EXPR. | to be overwhelmed (by weight, burden) |
| 咔嚓 | kāchā | ONOM. | snap |
| 助阵 | zhùzhèn | V./N. | to cheer/cheer |
| 偶然 | ǒurán | ADV. | by accident, by chance |
| 告诫 | gàojiè | V. | to warn |
| 不言自明 | bù yán zì míng | EXPR. | self-explanatory |

## Examples

甲：干嘛这么无精打采的？

乙：我给她发了很多短信，她都没回。

甲：不要<u>猴子捞月</u>瞎忙活啦，人家已经有新男朋友啦。

A: Why do you look so listless?

B: Well, I've texted her many times, but she's never responded.

A: Stop busying yourself for nothing: she's already hanging out with another boyfriend.

他们邀请信都发出去了，一句话不合便要分手，婚礼不得不被取消，这真是<u>猴子捞月</u>,场空啊。

After they sent out their invitations, they broke up because of an argument and canceled their wedding; whatever they have invested into the relationship has all gone down the drain.

# A Cunning Rabbit Has Three Burrows

| 狡 | 兔 | 三 | 窟 |
|---|---|---|---|
| *jiǎo* | *tù* | *sān* | *kū* |
| cunning, sly | rabbit, hare | three | cave, hole |

**Literal translation:** A cunning hare, three burrows.

**Meaning:** One must have multiple ways of protecting oneself.

This proverb comes from the chapter "Feng Yuan, a Retainer of Lord Mengchang" in *Strategies of the Warring States*, a book that relates the words and deeds of the political strategists of the time as well as the historical and social characteristics of the period. Its compiler is generally believed to be Liu Xiang, a government official, scholar, and writer of the Han dynasty (206 BCE–220 CE), but some scholars maintain that the true author is Kuai Tong, a strategist active at the end of the Qin dynasty (221–206 BCE).

## A Cunning Rabbit Has Three Burrows

During the Warring States period (475–221 BCE), it was a fad for aristocrats to keep retainers, which was considered to be not only a show of their economic and social status, but also a way of strengthening their political power. However, not all retainers were the same: some of them had real abilities and skills, while others were completely incompetent.

Lord Mengchang, an influential aristocrat, took Feng Xuan on as a retainer though the latter came to him in rags and scorned by everyone else. A year later, Lord Mengchang became chancellor to the state of Qi. By then, he had three thousand retainers. Despite his wealth, however, he still found it hard to feed them. Remembering the large fortune he had loaned to the people of Xue City, he dispatched Feng Xuan to collect the interest. Before his departure, Feng Xuan asked, "What would you like me to purchase for you with the money I collect?" Lord Mengchang answered, "Whatever you think I'm in need of."

Upon arriving in the city of Xue, Feng Xuan exempted those in poverty from paying the interest and burned their bonds as a testimony to Lord Mengchang's sincerity. As a result, everyone in Xue felt indebted to Lord Mengchang. When Feng Xuan returned, Lord Mengchang asked him what he had bought him. "Benevolence," Feng Xuan answered. When he learned what Feng Xuan had done, Lord Mengchang was extremely unhappy but refrained from exploding. He decided, however, to treat Feng Xuan as close as before.

Before long, Lord Mengchang was dismissed from his chancellorship and came to settle in Xue. Only then did he realize the true value of the benevolence that Feng Xuan had "bought" him, for the locals of Xue warmly welcomed him, making him feel at home. Lord Mengchang thanked Feng Xuan profusely, but the latter said, "Don't thank me yet. I'm still worried about your safety." Then he continued to explain, "A wily rabbit has three burrows to escape from its hunters. Your Excellency, at present you have only one. If the King of Qi wants to get rid of you, what would you do?" Lord Mengchang realized that he needed two more hideouts.

Feng Xuan went to see King Hui of Liang, and persuaded him to make Lord Mengchang a chancellor of Liang. However, Feng Xuan advised Lord Mengchang to stall on the invitation and wait. Soon the king of Qi learned about the king of Liang's interest in Lord Mengchang's talent. He lost no time in reinstating the ousted Lord Mengchang, unknowingly offering him a second "burrow." At Feng Xuan's advice, Lord Mengchang took the opportunity to ask the king of Qi that an ancestral temple be set up in Xue. To keep him from leaving, the king consented to his request. With the temple, Lord Mengchang secured his third "burrow." After the temple's completion, Feng Xuan said to Lord Mengchang, "With three burrows, you can really sleep with ease now."

This proverb teaches us that we must have multiple options to remain successful.

# 狡兔三窟

这条成语出自《战国策》中《冯谖客孟尝君》一文。《战国策》记述了战国时期纵横家的政治<u>主张</u>和言行<u>策略</u>，展示了战国时代的历史特点和社会<u>风貌</u>。一般认为汉朝官员学者和作家刘向是该书的<u>编撰</u>者，也有人认为秦末策士蒯通才是其真正的作者。

战国时期，<u>贵族豢养门客蔚然成风</u>。门客既是贵族们财富和地位的象征，又是他们借以<u>巩固</u>他们政治地位的工具。不过，门客有真才实学的，也有<u>滥竽充数</u>的。

大贵族孟尝君把一个叫冯谖的人收为门客，这个人初来的时候<u>破衣烂衫</u>，没有人瞧得起他。一年过后，孟尝君做了齐国的<u>宰相</u>。此时，他已门客三千，<u>尽管家底殷实</u>，但养活这么多人也感到<u>力不从心</u>。他想到了在薛城放过的大笔<u>高利贷</u>，于是派冯谖去把<u>利息</u>收回来。冯谖动身之前问孟尝君需不需要买点什么东西回来，孟尝君说，你看我缺什么就买什么吧。

冯谖一到薛地，就免除了那些穷人的<u>债务</u>，并以<u>烧毁</u>他们的债券为证。此举让薛地的人们对孟尝君<u>感恩戴德</u>。孟尝君见到冯谖后，问他买了什么东西回来，冯谖说："我给你买了'仁义'。"当孟尝了解到真相的时候，虽然<u>怒火</u>中烧，但还是隐忍下来，只是从此对冯谖不再像以前那样热情了。

直到后来，孟尝君被齐王<u>解职</u>，来到薛地<u>蛰居</u>，当地百姓把他像家人一样对待，他这才意识到冯谖为他买的仁义价值所在，连连感谢冯谖。冯谖说："你先别忙着谢我，你现在的<u>处境</u>依然让我担心。"他接着解释道："狡兔三窟，才不会被猎杀。您只有薛城一窟，万一齐国的国君要杀掉您，您怎么办？"孟尝君马上意识到，他还需要两窟。

冯谖于是去见梁惠王，说服他请孟尝君来帮他治理国家。然而，冯谖都嘱咐孟尝君先等一等，不要急于答应。梁国国君十分赏识孟尝君的消息，很快传到齐王的耳朵里，齐王赶紧请回孟尝君<u>官复原职</u>。按照冯谖的计策，孟尝君<u>趁势</u>要求齐王在薛地为他建立宗庙。齐王为留住孟尝君，便欣然答应了。薛地有了宗庙便成为孟尝君的第三个安全保障。等宗庙建好后，冯谖对孟尝君说："有了三个安身之地，以后您真可以<u>高枕无忧</u>啦。"

这条成语比喻，人要多些应变的办法，才能立于不败之地。

## Vocabulary

| Characters | Pinyin | Word Type | Translation |
| --- | --- | --- | --- |
| 主张 | zhǔ zhāng | N./V. | point of view; to stand for |
| 策略 | cèlüè | N. | strategy, tactic |
| 风貌 | fēngmào | N. | style, manner |
| 编撰 | biānzhuàn | V. | to compile, to edit |
| 豢养 | huànyǎng | V. | to keep, to look after (usually animals, but here also people) |
| 门客 | ménkè | N. | visitor; here: retainer |
| 蔚然成风 | wèi rán chéng fēng | EXPR. | to become a trend |
| 巩固 | gǒnggù | V. | to strengthen, consolidate |
| 滥竽充数 | lànyú chōngshù | EXPR. | to pretend (lit. pretending to play the flute to fill up the numbers) |
| 破衣烂衫 | pò yī làn shān | EXPR./N. | rags, ragged clothes |
| 宰相 | zǎixiàng | N. | prime minister (in ancient China) |
| 尽管 | jǐnguǎn | CONJ. | even though |
| 家底 | jiādǐ | N. | family wealth |
| 殷实 | yīnshí | ADJ. | well off, thriving |
| 力不从心 | lì bù cóng xīn | EXPR. | unable to do something as perfectly as one wishes |
| 高利贷 | gāolìdài | N. | high interest loan; a loan shark |
| 利息 | lìxī | N. | interest (on a loan) |
| 债务 | zhàiwù | N. | debt |
| 烧毁 | shāohuǐ | V. | to burn |
| 感恩戴德 | gǎn ēn dài dé | EXPR. | very grateful |
| 怒火 | nùhuǒ | N. | anger |
| 解职 | jiězhí | V. | to be fired |
| 谪居 | zhéjū | V. | to live in exile |
| 处境 | chǔjìng | N. | situation a person is in |
| 嘱咐 | zhǔfù | V. | to tell |
| 官复原职 | guān fù yuán zhí | EXPR. | to be reinstated to a former (official) post |
| 趁势 | chènshì | V. | to take advantage, to seize the opportunity |
| 高枕无忧 | gāo zhěn wú yōu | EXPR. | having no worries |

## Examples

在警方一路的搜捕中，发现嫌犯狡兔三窟，到处都有藏匿的地点。

While hunting for the suspect, the police found that he had many hide-outs, **like a smart rabbit with multiple burrows**.

甲：听说不少贪官把夫人和孩子都送到国外定居，他们一有风吹草动就会出逃。

乙：是的，这叫狡兔三窟啊。

A: I hear that many corrupt officials settle their families in foreign countries so that they can take off and join them if they feel something is wrong.

B: That's true. **They are like a cunning rabbit with three escape burrows.**

# Marking the Boat to Find Your Sword

| 刻 | 舟 | 求 | 剑 |
|---|---|---|---|
| kè | zhōu | qiú | jiàn |
| to carve | boat | to search | sword |

**Meaning:** Viewing or doing something in the same old way even though circumstances have changed.

This proverb derives from *Mr. Lü's Spring and Autumn Annals,* a book compiled by Lü Buwei (291–235 BCE) and his disciples. Lü was a prime minister of the state of Qin during the Warring States period of ancient China. His book was a summary of the contemporary philosophical thinking of Legalism, Confucianism, Mohism, and Daoism.

## Marking the Boat to Find Your Sword

Long ago, a man from the state of Chu dropped his sword into a river while traveling on a boat. Immediately, he asked a fellow traveler for a knife and unhurriedly carved a mark on the side of the moving boat where his sword had fallen.

When asked what he was doing, he said he wanted to remember where he dropped his sword so that when the boat pulled to shore, he would be able to fish it out. His fellow travelers could not help laughing at his remark, thinking he was being either silly or out of his mind.

When the boat reached the other bank of the river, the man jumped out where he had made the mark and fished for the sword in the knee-deep water. His fellow travelers and the people on the bank watched in amusement. The man didn't seem to understand that the boat had moved far away from where he had dropped the sword.

This proverb scoffs at those who act without regard for changes in circumstance.

# 刻舟求剑

这条谚语出自《吕氏春秋》，由吕不韦（291‐235 BCE）和他的弟子<u>编撰</u>。吕不韦是中国古代战国时期秦国的一位<u>丞相</u>。《吕氏春秋》对当时法家、儒家、墨家、道家等哲学思想做出了总结性的论述。

很久以前，一个楚国人乘船出游时，<u>不慎</u>把他的宝剑掉进河水里。他找同船的人要了一把刀，根据丢剑的位置，不慌不忙地在船帮上刻下一个<u>印记</u>。人们问他在做什么，他说他想记住宝剑坠落的位置，等船停下以后，再把剑给捞上来。听到这里，同船的人们都<u>忍俊不禁</u>，以为他不是个傻子就是个疯子。

船一<u>抵达</u>对岸，楚人就在船帮留下印记的地方跳进<u>齐膝</u>深的水中，开始<u>打捞</u>他的宝剑。船客以及<u>聚集</u>在岸边看热闹的人们都觉得很好笑。这个楚人哪里知道，船是移动的，而他那柄宝剑却是在原地不动的。

这条成语嘲笑的是那些不顾情况的变化，<u>我行我素</u>采取行动的人。

## Vocabulary

| Characters | Pinyin | Word Type | Translation |
|---|---|---|---|
| 刻 | kè | V. | to carve; to sculpt |
| 舟 | zhōu | N. | boat |
| 求 | qiú | V. | to seek; to look for; to retrieve |
| 剑 | jiàn | N. | sword |
| 编撰 | biānzhuàn | V. | to edit, to compile |
| 丞相 | chéngxiàng | N. | prime minister |
| 不慎 | bù shèn | ADV. | carelessly |
| 印记 | yìnjì | N. | mark |
| 忍俊不禁 | rěn jùn bù jīn | V. | to be unable to help but laugh, to succumb to laughter |
| 打捞 | dǎlāo | V. | to dredge, to fish out |
| 聚集 | jù jí | V. | to gather |
| 我行我素 | wǒ xíng wǒ sù | EXPR. | to do things one's own way |

## Examples

甲：看你精神恍惚，想什么哪？

乙：我还在为我们输掉选举而惋惜。

甲：我也是。可又一想，民众需求改变了，而我们还执著我们的理念，那不是刻舟求剑吗？

A: You are not quite yourself. What are you thinking?

B: I am still feeling sorry for the loss of the campaign.

A: Me, too. But on afterthought, if we still stick to our ideology while people's needs are changed, we are as good as the man who marks a moving boat and expects to retrieve the sword he has dropped in the water.

有些企业还在以来料加工的模式运作。在经济转型的今天，这无异于刻舟求剑。

Some enterprises are still operating in the mode of processing imported parts. In a time of economic transition, this practice is tantamount to marking a moving boat to locate a sword dropped overboard, acting in the same old way while the world is changing.

# A Fake Player in the Band

| 滥 | 竽 | 充 | 数 |
|---|---|---|---|
| làn | yú | chōng | shù |
| false, fallacious | an ancient wind instrument | to fill, to stuff | number, amount |

**Literal translation:** Pretending to play the *yu* to fill the numbers.

**Meaning:** Taking a position without real qualifications; putting on an act.

**English equivalent:** To be a makeweight.

This proverb stems from the chapter "The Seven Tactics" in the *Hanfeizi*, a philosophical text attributed to the eponymous Han Feizi, an influential politician and Legalist philosopher during the Warring States Period (475–221 BCE).

## A Fake Player in the Band

In the State of Qi, there was an idler known as Nanguo. One day, he was loafing around when he heard that the emperor had decreed the hiring of a large number of *yu* players, as the emperor loved listening to *yu* ensembles. The *yu* was a traditional Chinese musical instrument with a dozen bamboo pipes on top of a bowl-like copper base. The decree said specifically that if hired, a player would be paid handsomely every time he played in the band.

Unfortunately, Nanguo was by no means a *yu* player. In fact, he didn't know how to play any musical instrument at all. Yet he hated to let this lucrative opportunity slip by. He racked his brain for a way to get into the band. After all, he was not entirely worthless: everyone knew he was good at pretending. When he learned that one of the interviewers was as greedy for money as he was, he bribed the interviewer into recruiting him.

Soon the band was formed and gave its debut performance. Three hundred *yu* musicians sat in a square formation in the spacious court. Nanguo was among them, holding a *yu* to his mouth and mimicking every move of the other pipers.

His good fortune came to an end, however, when the emperor died the next year. His successor preferred the *yu* to be played solo, and Nanguo had to flee the country, knowing too well that deceiving an emperor was a capital crime.

The proverb satirizes someone who holds a position without adequate credentials. In modern use, it also criticizes the practice of making fakes of authentic or quality products in commerce.

# 滥竽充数

该成语出自一部哲学典籍《韩非子·内储说上七术》。作者韩非，是战国时期（公元前5-221年）颇具政治<u>影响力</u>的法家哲学家。

中国古代齐国里有个南郭先生，整天游手好闲、无所事事。一天，他正在街上闲逛的时候，突然听到国王<u>下旨</u>，说因为他喜欢听竽的合奏，所以需要<u>招募</u>一大批吹竽的能手。竽是一种古代的吹奏乐器，在一个铜质的斗上插有十二支竹苗。国王的诏书特别提到，凡是应聘者，每次合奏演出都会得到一笔<u>不菲</u>的<u>报酬</u>。

<u>遗憾</u>的是，别说吹竽，就连任何乐器南郭先生都没摸过。可是面对如此来钱的机会，他又怎能舍得错过呢。他想，自己也不是一无是处，毕竟大家都夸他会<u>模仿</u>。他<u>绞尽脑汁</u>想成为乐队的一员。当听到面试的一个官员像他一样贪财的时候，他便通过<u>贿赂</u>混进了乐队。

乐队很快成立起来，并开始了首场演出。三百个吹竽的乐师在朝廷里整整齐齐坐成一个大方阵。南郭先生双手把竽捧在脸前，<u>惟妙惟肖</u>地模仿着别人的每一个动作。可惜，好景不常，爱听竽合奏的国王第二年就<u>一命呜呼</u>了。即位的国王也爱听竽演奏，但必须是独奏。南郭先生不得不逃离了自己的王国。不逃，就要被控欺君之罪而<u>斩首</u>。

这个成语<u>讽刺</u>了那些没有真才实学却占着位子不做事的人。现在，该成语也用来批评在商业活动中<u>以次充好</u>、以假冒真的行为。

## Vocabulary

| Characters | Pinyin | Word Type | Translation |
|---|---|---|---|
| 影响力 | yǐngxiǎnglì | N. | influence |
| 下旨 | xiàzhǐ | V. | to issue an imperial decree |
| 招募 | zhāomù | V. | to recruit |
| 不菲 | bùfěi | ADJ. | considerable |
| 报酬 | bàochóu | N. | employment compensation, remuneration |
| 遗憾 | yíhàn | N./ADJ. | pity, regret; unfortunate, regretful |
| 绞尽脑汁 | jiǎo jìn nǎozhī | V. | to try one's best to think of something, to rack one's brain |
| 贿赂 | huì lù | V. | to bribe |
| 惟妙惟肖 | wéi miào wéi xiāo | EXPR. | in a manner mimicking life, pretending |
| 模仿 | mófǎng | V. | to mimic, to copy, to imitate |
| 一命呜呼 | yī mìng wūhū | EXPR. | to die, to breathe one's last |
| 斩首 | zhǎnshǒu | V. | to behead |
| 讽刺 | fěngcì | V./N. | to satirize, to mock; satire, irony |
| 以次充好 | yǐcì chōnghǎo | EXPR. | to produce a fake product, to sell an inferior product at high prices |

## Examples

我看这些参赛作品，除少数是真才实学，其他都是滥竽充数。

In my opinion, only a small number of the entries in the contest are products of solid research. The rest are all **fakes**.

甲：你买什么了？

乙：从自由市场买了橘子。可是你看，有几个坏的，真气人。

甲：嗨，这是滥竽充数啊。

A: What did you get?

B: I've bought some oranges at the free market. But you see, there are some bad ones among the goods ones. It's really annoying.

A: Well, the peddler was **cheating by mixing them together**.

# Aspiring to Become a Dragon

| 鲤鱼 | 跳 | 龙 | 门 |
|---|---|---|---|
| lǐ yú | tiào | lóng | mén |
| carp | to jump, to leap | dragon | door, gate |

**Literal translation:** Carp leaping over Dragon Gate.

**Meaning:** Getting promoted to a higher office; striving for success despite great difficulties.

This proverb comes from a folktale about carp leaping over Mount Dragon Gate to get to a beautiful lake on the other side. The folktale is believed to have taken shape sometime in the early Western Han dynasty (206 BCE–9 CE). According to a later historical text, "carp leaping over Dragon Gate" had already become a well-known saying by the Eastern Han period (25–220 CE).

鲤鱼跳龙门

## **Aspiring to Become a Dragon**

The carp living in the Mengjin section of the Yellow (Huang) River heard of a beautiful and miraculous place at Mount Dragon Gate. They yearned to visit it despite the distance of a thousand miles. One day, they set off. Passing through the Luo River, they eventually arrived at Mount Dragon Gate. Blocking the Yellow River, this mountain created a giant, magic lake on the other side. It was believed to contain a magnificent dragon palace in it. There lived the Dragon King and his children and grandchildren. It was into this lake that the carp really wanted to get. Looking up from the water, the carp saw Mount Dragon Gate soaring high. Disheartened, they gazed with wide-open eyes from the shallow water at the foot of the cliff, gasping for air in the waves bouncing back from the shore. Unable to move forward and yet having come too far to return, they didn't know what to do.

Suddenly, a big red carp bolted into the air, swung around, and fell back into the water facing its buddies. Raising its voice, Big Red Carp said, "I've got an idea! Let's leap over Mount Dragon Gate."

"What? Who could jump over such a high mountain?" said one carp. "What if we fail to leap over and fall to our death?" chimed in another. The carp started raising questions one after another. The more questions they asked, the less confident they became. Undaunted, Big Red Carp said, "Well, since I made the suggestion, I'll try it first."

It swam back a quarter of a mile and, with a big wag of its tail, turned around and charged full speed toward Mount Dragon Gate. Just before hitting the mountainside, Big Red Carp sprang up with all its might and soared into the sky. Out of the blue, a thunderbolt caught Big Red Carp and a fireball burned off its tail. Enduring the pain, Big Red Carp charged forward, taking advantage of the momentum of his jump. It finally flew over the mountain and fell into the lake. Magic happened: the moment Big Red Carp touched the water, it turned into a dragon.

Bolstered by the courage that Big Red Carp had demonstrated, those in the Yellow River went into action. Eventually, many of them succeeded and became dragons themselves. Those who failed became the ancestors of present-day carp in the Yellow River. Falling back onto the surface of the water left a visible black scar on their head, and their posterity still bears the same mark today.

This proverb has two meanings. One is getting promoted and becoming prosperous; the other is to strive forward despite great difficulties.

# 鲤鱼跳龙门

这则成语起源于鲤鱼跳龙门的故事,而故事则成型于西汉(公元前206 - 公元9年)早年,并于东汉(公元25 - 220年)时期开始盛传。

生活在河南孟津黄河里的鲤鱼们听说千里之外有个叫龙门山的地方,那里<u>风光旖旎</u>而又神奇。虽有千里之遥,它们还是想去看一看。一天,它们出发了。经过洛河最终来到龙门山。该山把黄河<u>阻断</u>,在另一边形成一个巨大而又神奇的湖,据说湖里有座辉煌的龙宫,是龙王和龙子龙孙出没的地方。鲤鱼们正是想到那个湖里去的。可是,从黄河水里抬头望去,龙门山高高<u>耸立</u>着,鲤鱼们的心一下子沉到了河底:这么高,怎么过去呀!它们挤在龙门山脚下的水里,睁大着眼睛,大口大口地吸吮着浪花中的空气,<u>进退两难</u>,<u>不知所措</u>。

忽然,一条大红鲤鱼跃出水面,在空中<u>矫健</u>地转了个身,落进水里面对鱼群,提高嗓门说:"我有个主意!咱们跳过这座龙门山!"

"山那么高,谁能跳得过去呀?""再说了,要是跳不好,摔死了怎么办?"鲤鱼们你一句我一句地议论着,越说越没了底气。大红鲤鱼毫不<u>气馁</u>,说:"既然主意是我出的,那我就先去试一试吧。"

于是,它逆水回游了半里地,尾巴一甩转过身来,憋足浑身的力量,对着龙门山就冲了过来。就要撞到山脚那一刻,只见它纵身一跃,像离弦的箭一样冲出水面,飞到半空的时候,云中突然出现一串火球,其中一个火球把大红鲤鱼的尾巴给烧掉了。它忍着剧痛,继续<u>任凭惯性</u>推着它的前半身前行,终于越过了龙门山,落到山南的湖中。结果<u>奇</u>迹发生了,它一落入水中,就变成了一条龙。

大红鲤鱼的勇敢行为,鼓舞了山这边黄河里的鲤鱼们,它们开始行动起来。最后,它们中有很多跳过去变成了龙。而那些没能跳过去的鲤鱼,从空中落下来的时候,头部碰到坚硬的水面后落下一个黑疤。直到今天,这个黑疤还长在黄河鲤鱼的额头上呢。

这条成语,现在有两重意思:一个是比喻升官发财,<u>飞黄腾达</u>;另一个则是比喻逆流前进,奋发向上。

## Vocabulary

| Characters | Pinyin | Word Type | Translation |
| --- | --- | --- | --- |
| 风光旖旎 | fēngguāng yǐnǐ | ADJ. | beautiful (particularly used to describe scenery) |
| 阻断 | zǔduàn | V. | to block |
| 辉煌 | huīhuáng | ADJ. | splendid, glorious |
| 耸立 | sǒnglì | V. | to tower above, to stand tall |
| 进退两难 | jìn tùi liǎng nán | EXPR. | to be in a dilemma, stuck between a rock and a hard place |
| 不知所措 | bù zhī suǒ cuò | EXPR. | not know what to do (in order to solve a problem) |
| 矫健 | jiǎojiàn | ADV./ADJ. | vigorous, strong |
| 气馁 | qìněi | V. | to be discouraged |
| 任凭 | rènpíng | CONJ. | no matter what, despite |
| 惯性 | guànxìng | N. | inertia, momentum |
| 奇迹 | qí jī | N. | miracle |
| 飞黄腾达 | fēi huáng téngdá | EXPR. | to be successful in one's official career |

## Examples

农民老张的儿子大学毕业留校任教，终于<u>鲤鱼跳龙门</u>了，方圆十里谁都羡慕。

When his son graduated from college got a job teaching at the same university, farmer Lao Zhang **became an object of envy** for everyone within a ten-mile radius.

自从他结交了老板的女儿后，真可说是<u>鲤鱼跳龙门</u>，神气得很。

His acquaintance with the boss's daughter has made him arrogant. He's acting like a big shot, as if he's **a carp that leaped over the Dragon Gate and became a dragon himself.**

# The Man from Qi Who Worries About the Sky

| 杞 | 人 | 忧 | 天 |
|---|---|---|---|
| Qǐ | rén | yōu | tiān |
| a Chinese state from the sixteenth to the fifth centuries BCE in modern-day Henan Province | person | to worry | sky, heaven |

**Literal translation:** A man from the state of Qi worries about the sky.

**Meaning:** To overact to groundless worries.

**English equivalent:** Chicken Little.

The story behind this proverb comes from the Liezi, a Daoist text allegedly written by Lie Yukou, a Chinese philosopher of the state of Zheng who lived around the fifth century BCE.

## The Man from Qi Who Worries About the Sky

There once lived a man in the State of Qi, who had a habit of worrying for no reason. One day, he feared that the sky might fall. Another day he dreaded that the earth would sink. He was so scared that he could neither sleep nor eat. His neighbors began to worry about him. They came over to tell him that the sky was simply made of the air that he was living in every day, so there was nothing to be afraid of. Unconvinced, the man of Qi asked, "If the sky were formed of air, how could it carry the sun, the moon, and the stars? Wouldn't they fall at some point?" At his question, the neighbors tried to explain and comfort him. They told him that those celestial bodies were made of air, too, the only difference being that they were illuminated. Even if they did fall, they would be harmless.

The man of Qi, however, was still terrified at the thought that he might sink with the earth. His neighbors again tried their best to allay his fear, arguing that the earth was nothing but an accumulation of solid dirt. "It's there for you to step on no matter where you go," they added, "so what's there to be scared of?" On hearing this, the man of Qi broke into a smile, his first in a long time.

This proverb reminds us that many of our fears are unfounded and not worth agonizing over.

# 杞人忧天

这则寓言出自《列子》，是一部道家典籍，据说由郑人哲学家列御寇（约公元前五世纪）所著。

　　从前有个杞国人，常常忧心忡忡。今天怕天要塌下来，明天又担心地要陷下去，结果弄得寝食不安。他的邻居为他感到很揪心，于是就过来安慰他，告诉他说，天是由空气构成的，他每天就生活在空气中，没有什么好担心的。这个杞人半信半疑地问道，"要是天是由空气构成的，那它怎能承载得了日月星辰呢？难道它们不会坠落下来吗？"对他提出的问题，邻居们尽力加以解释，以求让他安心。他们说，日月星辰也都是由气体组成的，只不过会发光而已。即使掉下来，也不会把人砸伤。

　　然而，杞人依然害怕会陷到地里去，邻居们告诉他不要害怕，因为大地不过是由一块一块的土地组合而成。"不管走到哪儿，你都会踩到它。所以，这又有什么可害怕的呢？"听完这话，这个杞人咧开嘴笑了。他很长时间没有笑过了。

　　这个谚语提醒我们，我们的许多恐惧是毫无根据的，不值得为其而痛苦。

## Vocabulary

| Characters | Pinyin | Word Type | Translation |
|---|---|---|---|
| 忧心忡忡 | yōu xīn chōng chōng | EXPR. | worried and anxious |
| 塌 | tā | V. | to collapse |
| 陷 | xiàn | V. | to sink; to entrap |
| 寝 | qǐn | V. | to sleep |
| 揪心 | jiūxīn | ADJ. | worried |
| 安慰 | ānwèi | V. | to console, to comfort |
| 构成 | gòuchéng | V. | to constitute, to make up |
| 半信半疑 | bàn xìn bàn yí | EXPR. | to be uncertain as to what to believe |
| 承载 | chéngzài | V. | to carry |
| 踩 | cǎi | V. | to step on; to tread |

## Examples

所谓玛雅人2012年是世界末日的预言，是现代人的误解，不要杞人忧天。

The so-called Mayan Prophecy that predicts 2012 as the end of the world is the contemporary world's misunderstanding of what the Mayans were saying, **so let's not worry ourselves unnecessarily**.

甲: 跟我去游泳馆游泳去吧?

乙: 不去，听说在游泳池游泳会染病的。

甲: 别杞人忧天啦，游泳池都是消毒过的，很安全。

A: Are you going to the indoor swimming pool with me?

B: No way. I hear that you may get diseases from the pool.

A: Come on! **Don't scare yourself without reason**. All pools are safe because they're sanitized.

# A Horse Lost Is a Stable Gained

| 塞 | 翁 | 失 | 马 |
|---|---|---|---|
| sài | wēng | shī | mǎ |
| a place of strategic importance | old man | to lose | horse |

| 焉 | 知 | 非 | 福 |
|---|---|---|---|
| yān | zhī | fēi | fú |
| how, why, where? (rhetorical question) | to know, to realize | to not be, not | good fortune, blessing |

**Literal translation:** An old frontiersman [Sai Weng] loses a horse, but how do we know it's not luck?

**Meaning:** A bad incident may be a blessing in disguise or vice versa.

**English equivalent:** A blessing in disguise.

This proverb stems from an allegory in the Chinese philosophical classic the *Huainanzi*, attributed to the renowned historical figure Liu An (179–122 BCE).

## A Horse Lost Is a Stable Gained

In ancient times, there was an old man who lived in northern China, bordering the habitat of the Xiongnu, a nomadic people who raided China from time to time. Wars were frequent. The old man, like many in the region, made a living breeding war horses. One day, the best of the old man's horses got loose and strayed across the border. His neighbors, thinking that the old man must be devastated, came over to comfort him, only to find that he was alright. Instead of being unhappy, he told his neighbors that this might be a blessing in disguise.

Sure enough, a few months later, his horse galloped back, bringing with it a band of horses from a Xiongnu stable. The neighbors then went to congratulate the old man, who said, to their surprise, that good luck might turn into bad, so there was nothing to be too happy about. His words proved true a few days later, when his son was bucked off one of the Xiongnu' horses and got injured. The old man, however, saw the accident in a positive light, to the bewilderment of his neighbors again.

A bloody war soon broke out between the Chinese and the Xiongnu. Casualties were terribly high on both sides. But due to his injury, the old man's son was spared from being drafted and killed in action. All these turns of events testified to the old man's philosophy that fortune might bring misfortune, or the other way around.

This proverb suggests that we react with moderation to life's ups and downs since we never know when something unwanted might be a blessing in disguise.

# 塞翁失马，焉知非福

这则成语源自中国的哲学典籍《淮南子》中的一个寓言。《淮南子》的作者据说是刘安（公元前179–122年），一个传奇人物。

古时候，与游牧的匈奴人接壤的北方边塞，住着一位老汉。匈奴人不断骚扰边境，与汉人的战争经常发生。像边塞许多人一样，老汉以饲养战马为生。一天，老汉最好的一匹马脱缰逃过了边境，邻居们都认为老汉会很难过。于是纷纷过来安慰他，却发现他气定神闲地说："丢马说不定还是件好事呢。"

几个月后，他的话果然应验了：不仅自己的马跑了回来，而且后边还跟着一群匈奴人的马。邻居们于是又过来祝贺老汉。可老汉居然说，好事也许会变成坏事的，有什么值得祝贺？他的话，没过几天竟然又被一件事给印证了，他儿子骑的一匹匈奴马尥蹶子把他摔伤。可老汉并不认为这事很糟糕。邻居听了，再次感到莫名其妙。

不久，一场血腥的战争又在匈奴与汉人之间爆发了。边塞地区的年轻人十之八九战死在疆场。老汉的儿子由于摔伤，侥幸逃过征兵，从而保住了性命。这一连串的事件，一再证明了老汉的这个信条：祸兮福所倚，福兮祸所伏。

这则成语表明，我们对生活的跌宕起伏大可不必做出过激的反应，毕竟我们无法预料什么时候会祸倚之于福，什么时候又会福伏之于祸。

## Vocabulary

| Characters | Pinyin | Word Type | Translation |
|---|---|---|---|
| 边塞 | biānsài | N. | frontier fortress |
| 失踪 | shīzōng | V. | to go missing, to disappear |
| 战马 | zhànmǎ | N. | war horse |
| 游牧 | yóumù | V. | to live a nomadic life |
| 接壤 | jiērǎng | V. | to border |
| 骚扰 | sāorǎo | V. | to harass |
| 以…为生 | yǐ...wéishēng | EXPR. | to live on (doing something) |
| 脱缰 | tuōjiāng | V. | (of a horse) to run fast out of fear |
| 印证 | yìnzhèng | V. | to confirm |
| 尥蹶子 | liàojuězi | V. | (of a horse) to buck |
| 莫名其妙 | mòmíng qí miào | EXPR. | to be baffled |
| 血腥 | xuèxīng | ADJ. | bloody |
| 侥幸 | jiǎoxìng | ADV. | luckily |

## Examples

我知道你和女朋友分手了，别难过。说不定是<u>塞翁失马</u>，焉知非福，你也许会找到一位更适合你的姑娘。

I know you and your girlfriend broke up, but don't feel too bad. **It may be a blessing in disguise** because now you might meet someone more compatible with you.

他起晚了，错过了航班。当他后来知道那班飞机不知所踪的时候，庆幸自己竟是<u>塞翁失马</u>，安知非福。

He got up late and missed the flight but realized it was **a blessing in disguise** when he later learned that the plane went missing.

# Three People Can Create a Tiger

| 三 | 人 | 成 | 虎 |
|---|---|---|---|
| sān | rén | chéng | hǔ |
| three | person, people | to create, make | tiger |

三
人
成
虎

**Meaning:** A lie or a rumor, if repeated often enough, will be accepted as truth.

This proverb derives from the "Wei State Strategies" chapter of the *Strategies of the Warring States*, allegedly compiled by Liu Xiang (77–6 BCE), a scholar and government offical of the Han dynasty.

## Three People Can Create a Tiger

The king of Wei wanted to befriend the king of Zhao. He decided to send his heir-apparent to Handan, the capital of Zhao, to become a hostage, which was a custom at the time to guarantee the implementation of a political deal between two states. The king of Wei asked his favored minister Pang Gong to accompany his son.

Pang Gong knew that his political enemies at home would slander him before the king during his absence. Therefore, he asked the king, "Your Majesty, if someone told you there was a tiger prowling in the street, would you believe him?"

"Certainly not," said the king categorically. "How can there be a tiger in the street?"

"And if another person came to tell the same story, would you believe him?"

"Well, I would take it with a grain of salt."

"What if still another came with the same story?"

"Then," said the king, "I would definitely think that they were telling the truth."

Pang Gong said, "Now that I am leaving for the capital of Zhao with the heir-apparent, I'm afraid there may be more than three people trying to stab me in the back. I hope that Your Majesty won't take their lies seriously."

The king of Wei said, "Rest assured, I won't be taken in so easily."

After Pang Gong left, people indeed began slandering him. The king didn't believe them at first, but as the number of backstabbers increased, the king grew more credulous despite his previous assurance to Pang Gong. When Pang Gong returned to the state of Wei, his fear had become a reality: The king would not trust him anymore.

This proverb reminds us not to believe something just because we're hearing it from a lot of sources, and not to pass on unverified information either, lest we lead others to think it's true.

# 三人成虎

这则成语出自《战国策·魏策》。该书作者据说是汉代一位叫刘向（公元前77－6年）的学者和朝臣。

魏国国君想与赵国国君交好，遂决定将太子送去赵国国都邯郸做人质。这是那时的惯例，目的是要确保两国之间达成的政治交易能够顺利进行。魏王派他最信赖的大臣庞恭随行。

庞恭深知，他离开魏国以后，他的政敌会进谗言诋毁他。于是就问魏王："陛下，如果有人告诉您说街上有只老虎，您信吗？"

"当然不啦，"国王说得很干脆，"街上怎么会有老虎呢？"

"如果又来一个人说有老虎，您还信吗？"

"嗯，我会考虑一下。"

"要是再来一个人说有虎呢？"

魏王说，"那我当然会认为他们讲的都是真话啦。"

庞恭说，"我现在要陪太子去做人质了，在背后讲我坏话的，恐怕不会只有三个人。还望陛下明察，不要把谗言当作真话。"

魏王说道，"你放心，我哪会轻易上当呢。"

然而，庞恭走后，人们便开始向魏王进谗言陷害他。魏王开始并不在意，但是，随着进谗言的人多起来，魏王果然就信以为真了。等庞恭回到魏国的时候，他的担心已经变成了事实：魏王再也不信任他了。

这则成语告诫我们，不要因为听到的消息来源多就以为是事实。也不要传播不实的消息，以免误导他人。

## Vocabulary

| Characters | Pinyin | Word Type | Translation |
|---|---|---|---|
| 人人 | rénrén | N. | everybody |
| 成人 | chéngrén | V./N. | to become of age; adult |
| 遂 | suì | ADV. | then, thereupon |
| 人质 | rénzhì | N. | hostage |
| 信赖 | xìnlài | V. | to trust |
| 政敌 | zhèngdí | N. | political enemy |
| 谗言 | chányán | N. | slander |
| 诋毁 | dǐhuǐ | V. | to defame, to vilify |
| 明察 | chányán | V. | to perceive |
| 轻易 | qīngyì | ADV. | easily, readily |
| 上当 | shàngdàng | V. | to be taken in |

## Examples

虽然谣言总会被识破，但是短期内，<u>三人成虎</u>，还是会造成不小的危害。

A rumor will eventually prove false, but it can be very harmful in the short term if **many people believe it's true**.

现在，有很多人在社交网站上有意无意地转载一些假消息。就怕<u>三人成虎</u>，谎言经过多人转载，最终会让人们信以为真的。

These days a lot of people are knowingly or unknowingly forwarding fake news on the internet. The problem is, as the story goes, **if three people claim there's a tiger prowling on the street**, people will believe it's true. The same happens to the fake news being spread on the internet.

# Waiting for Another Hare to Come Your Way

| 守 | 株 | 待 | 兔 |
|---|---|---|---|
| shǒu | zhū | dài | tù |
| to guard | a tree stump | to wait | hare, rabbit |

**Literal translation:** Guarding a tree stump and wait for a hare.

**Meaning:** Waiting for a lucky break without putting in any effort.

This proverb originates from the section "Five Vermin: A Pathological Analysis of Politics" of the *Hanfeizi* by Han Feizi (c. 280–233 BCE), the eponymous Legalist philosopher of the Warring States Period. The book comprises a synthesis of legal theories up to his time.

## Waiting for Another Hare to Come Your Way

In the state of Song, there was a farmer who often dreamed of a windfall that would spare him the backbreaking toil in the fields. One day, he was tilling a plot when a hare suddenly darted by as if it was desperately fleeing from a beast of prey. It rushed so fast and so recklessly that it crashed into a tree stump, broke its neck, and died. The farmer took the hare home and cooked it up for a delicious meal. He had never imagined that a fat hare would simply drop into his lap like that. From the next day on, the farmer, casting his farm tools aside, started sitting a short distance from the stump, waiting for another hare to bump into it so that he could have another good meal without putting in any effort.

Day after day, month after month, he went to the field to simply wait instead of doing any farm work. He waited and waited until weeds took over his field, but never had another hare run by at breakneck speed. Soon, winter set in. The farmer finally understood that an accident was an accident, and he should not have bet his livelihood on haphazard incidents. Unfortunately, his revelation came too late because he was not growing a single crop, and the season was coming to an end.

This proverb satirizes those who expect to succeed by serendipity instead of diligence. In modern times, it means lying in wait for someone to come by or for something to come to pass.

# 守株待兔

这条成语出自《韩非子》的"五蠹"。作者韩非（约公元前280 - 233），也被称为韩非子，是战国时期最伟大的法家哲学家。与作者同名的《韩非子》一书对截至他那个时代的法律进行了论述。

宋国有个农民，经常<u>梦想</u>着发财，以便从<u>繁重</u>的劳作中解脱出来。一天，他正在地里劳作的时候，突然<u>冲</u>过来一只野兔，似在<u>拼命</u>逃脱后面的<u>追杀</u>。因为<u>慌不择路</u>，一头撞在地里的一颗树桩上，折断了脖颈，倒地死去。农夫捡起野兔拿回家，做成一顿美餐。他从没想到，居然可以<u>不劳而获</u>地得到一只肥美的野兔。从此以后，这个农民便把手里的农具扔在一边，在离树桩不远的地方坐下来，静静地等待着下一只可怜的野兔跑过来，撞死在树桩下，好让他再次<u>不费吹灰之力</u>地品尝到野兔的美味。

他就这样<u>日复一日</u>、<u>月复一月</u>地<u>等</u>待着，一直等到地里长满野草，也没抓到一只野兔。不久，冬天来临，农民才<u>恍然大悟</u>：起初的那次幸运纯属<u>偶然</u>，他实在不该赌上一年的<u>生计</u>。可惜，<u>颗粒无收</u>的他明白得太晚了。

这条成语讽刺的是，那些把成功寄望于偶然而非勤奋的人。

## Vocabulary

| Characters | Pinyin | Word Type | Translation |
| --- | --- | --- | --- |
| 五蠹 | wǔdú | N. | (Chinese mythology) five venomous pests: scorpion, snake, centipede, toad, and spider |
| 梦想 | mèngxiǎng | N./V. | (day)dream; to dream, to daydream |
| 发财 | fācái | V. | to make a fortune |
| 繁重 | fánzhòng | ADJ. | (of workload) heavy |
| 解脱 | jiětuō | V. | to get free from |
| 劳作 | láozuò | N./V. | toil, to toil |
| 冲 | chōng | V. | to charge forward |
| 拼命 | pīnmìng | ADJ. | desperate |
| 慌不择路 | huāng bù zé lù | EXPR. | so hurriedly as to disregard where to flee |
| 不劳而获 | bù láo ér huò | V. | to get something without working for it |
| 不费吹灰之力 | bù fèi chuī huī zhī lì | EXPR. | as easy as pie, without any effort |
| 日复一日 | rì fù yī rì | ADV. | day after day |
| 等待 | děngdài | V. | to wait |
| 恍然大悟 | huǎngrán dàwù | EXPR. | to come to a sudden realization |
| 纯属 | chúnshǔ | ADJ. | pure and simple, outright |
| 颗粒无收 | kēlì wú shōu | EXPR. | nothing is reaped at harvest time |

## Examples

警察在嫌疑人寓所周围<u>守株待兔</u>，只等他出来时把他抓捕。

The police officers were **lying in wait** for the suspect to come out of his residence so they could arrest him.

甲：我好久没有工作了，不知什么时候才会有机会去工作。
乙：这样天天宅在家里<u>守株待兔</u>，工作的机会回来找你吗？

A: I haven't worked for a long time. I'm not sure when there's a job opportunity.
B: Well, you need to look for it instead of **waiting for it** at home. Are you expecting a job opportunity to come to you?

# Catching a Cicada, Blind to the Oriole

| 螳螂 | 捕 | 蝉 | 黄雀 | 在 | 后 |
|---|---|---|---|---|---|
| *tángláng* | *bǔ* | *chán* | *huángquè* | *zài* | *hòu* |
| (praying) mantis | to catch, to seize | cicada | oriole | at | behind, after |

**Literal translation:** A praying mantis catches a cicada; an oriole is behind him.

**Meaning:** Coveting something so single-mindedly that you're blind to everything else, including dangers lurking around you.

This proverb comes from a fable that first appeared in the chapter "Mountain Trees" in the Zhuangzi, a classic attributed to *Zhuangzi* (c. 369–286 BCE), a Chinese thinker, philosopher, and a man of letters, as well as a leading Daoist of the Warring States period. Because he inherited and developed the thinking of Laozi, his name is often associated with the latter as "Lao-Zhuang." Historian Liu Xiang (77–6 BCE) told the story in his *Garden of Stories* based on Zhuangzi's fable.

螳螂捕蝉，黄雀在后

## Catching a Cicada, Blind to the Oriole

The king of the State of Wu decided to launch an attack against the State of Chu, but his ministers adamantly objected that the likelihood of defeating Chu was high alright, but other states might grab the opportunity to attack their state while its troops were away. The consequences would be unthinkable. But the stubborn king decreed that whoever tried to dissuade him from attacking the State of Chu be put to death.

One of the king's young chamberlains was determined to talk him out of his decision. Aware that the king would not be easily swayed by someone as young as himself and that he would face sure death if he failed, he knew he had to figure out a smart way to bring the king around. Therefore, with pellets in his robe pockets and a slingshot in his hand, he started roaming the garden in the rear of the palace. Seeing him acting like this for three days, the king could no longer reign in his curiosity. He stopped the young chamberlain and asked, "I've been watching you wandering in the garden while your clothes are dampened by the dew. What on earth have you been doing?"

The young chamberlain answered, "I found a cicada singing sadly while sucking the sap of a tree in the garden. While doing so, it was unaware of a praying mantis arching behind ready to snatch it with its front legs. But the mantis, meanwhile, was unaware of an oriole lurking nearby prepared to make off with it at any moment."

"And the oriole was oblivious of you lurking behind it ready to shoot it with a slingshot, right?" The king seemed to know where the young chamberlain was going with this. "Yes," replied the young chamberlain. "The oriole was so focused on the mantis that there's no way it could sense that I was aiming my slingshot at it. The cicada, the mantis, and the oriole—all were so obsessed with the prize under their noses that they neglected the danger behind them."

Hearing the young chamberlain's reasoning, the king mumbled with dawning comprehension, "That's true! That's true! What you said makes profound sense!" He then gave up the idea of attacking the state of Chu right away.

This proverb teaches us that if we make decisions based solely on our immediate interests and fail to think carefully about the bigger picture and hidden consequences, we risk suffering catastrophic outcomes.

# 螳螂捕蝉，黄雀在后

这条成语最早出现在《庄子·山木》一书中，作者庄周，亦称庄子（约前369年－前286年），是战国时期著名的思想家、哲学家、文学家，也是道家学派的代表人物、老子思想的继承和发展者，后世将他与老子并称为"老庄"。西汉史学家、文学家刘向（前77年－前6年）在其《说苑·正谏》一书中讲述了下面这个故事，故事借用了庄子关于螳螂捕蝉的寓言。

吴王准备出兵攻打楚国，<u>遭到</u>了一些大臣的反对。大臣们认为，攻打楚国虽然取胜的希望很大，但如果其他诸侯国<u>趁虚而入</u>，后果将<u>不堪设想</u>。可是吴王<u>固执</u>地说："谁敢再来<u>劝阻</u>我，我就处死他！"

吴王的<u>侍从</u>中有个人下定决心要劝谏吴王。可是，一来他年纪轻轻，说话难以让吴王信服；二来吴王已<u>经把话说死</u>，顶风行事，等于白白送命。看来，要用巧妙的办法才能达到劝阻的目的。于是他就怀里揣着弹丸，手里拿着弹弓，在皇宫的后院里一连<u>转悠</u>了三天。到了第四天早晨，吴王见他还在后院里转悠，终于忍不住，就拦住他好奇地问道，"我看见你每天在这里转来转去的，衣服都让露水打湿了，你到底是在干什么呢？"

年轻的侍从回答说："我看到园子里有棵树，高处的树枝上有只蝉，在那儿一边凄凉地叫着一边吮吸着露水，却浑然不知身后有只弓身举爪的螳螂正在准备去<u>捉</u>它。而螳螂也没注意到有只黄雀躲在它的旁边，正伸长着脖子想要啄食它。"

"那只黄雀也不知道你躲在树下，拿着弹弓正要去打它，对不对？"吴王似乎知道年轻侍从接下来想要说什么了。年轻人赶紧回答说："是呀，黄雀正在<u>聚精会神</u>地准备啄食螳螂，哪里会注意到我拿着弹弓在<u>瞄准</u>它呢？蝉、螳螂、黄雀，都一心想着眼前的利益，所以忽视了自己身后的<u>祸患</u>啊！"

听了年轻侍从的这番话，吴王恍然大悟，连声说："对！对！你讲得太有道理了！"说完<u>当即</u>打消了攻打楚国的念头。

这条寓言般的成语，<u>告诫</u>人们不要为了眼前的利益而考虑不周，反而会失去更大的利益。

## Vocabulary

| Characters | Pinyin | Word Type | Translation |
| --- | --- | --- | --- |
| 遭到 | zāodào | V. | to meet with (something negative) |
| 趁虚而入 | chén xū ér rù | EXPR. | to take advantage of a weak spot (and enter) |
| 不堪设想 | bù kān shè xiǎng | ADJ. | unthinkable, too horrible to contemplate (used to describe a result or outcome) |
| 固执 | gùzhí | ADJ./ADV. | stubborn; stubbornly |
| 劝阻 | quànzǔ | N. | to dissuade |
| 侍从 | shìcóng | N. | chamberlain |
| 劝谏 | quànjiǎn | V. | to plead for rectification |
| 把话说死 | bǎ huà shuō sǐ | EXPR. | to make what's said the final word |
| 转悠 | zhuàn yōu | V. | to loiter |
| 露水 | lùshuǐ | N. | dew |
| 吸允 | xīyǔn | V. | to suck |
| 捉 | zhuō | V. | to catch |
| 聚精会神 | jù jīng huì shén | EXPR. | to be focused, attentive |
| 瞄准 | miáozhǔn | V. | to aim at |
| 祸患 | huòhuàn | N. | (usually hidden) disaster |
| 当即 | dāngjì | ADV. | immediately, right away |
| 告诫 | gàojiè | V. | to warn, caution |

# Catching a Cicada, Blind to the Oriole ∗ 螳螂捕蝉，黄雀在后

## Examples

小偷只顾着偷东西，却没有想到<u>螳螂捕蝉，黄雀在后</u>，警察已经在外头等着逮捕他了。

Focusing on robbing, the thief **was oblivious to** the police officers outside waiting to arrest him.

甲：抗日战争初期，毛泽东用一个成语告诫蒋介石不要打边区。

乙：什么成语？

甲：<u>螳螂捕蝉，黄雀在后</u>。

乙：什么意思呢？

甲：很显然，如果国军攻打红军的话，日本侵略军就会像黄雀一样攻击国军。

A: During the Second Sino-Japanese War, Mao Zedong used a proverb to warn Chiang Kai-shek against attacking the Communist-occupied border region.

B: What proverb?

A: "**The mantis stalking a cicada unaware of the oriole behind.**"

B: So, what does it mean?

A: Apparently, if the Nationalist Army had attacked the Red Army, the Japanese invaders would have attacked the Nationalist Army.

# Crossing the River in the Same Boat

| 同 | 舟 | 共 | 济 |
|---|---|---|---|
| tóng | zhōu | gòng | jì |
| same | boat | common, general | to ferry; to cross a river |

**Literal translation:** On the same boat crossing together.

**Meaning:** Working closely together to overcome difficulties.

This proverb originates from *The Art of War*, authored by Sun Wu (544–496 BCE). A famous war strategist of the Spring and Autumn period, Sun Wu has been revered as Master Sun (Sunzi or Sun Tzu).

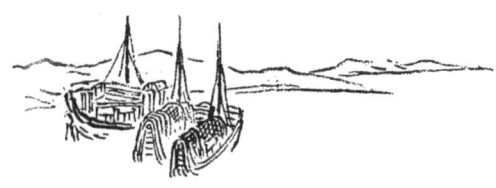

# Crossing the River in the Same Boat

One day, a man asked Sun Wu how to arrange troops so that they could be invincible. Sun Wu answered, "To arrange troops, one must have in mind a snake striking back at a hunter. Troops must be arranged to be maneuverable as an integrated whole that can take care of its front and rear like a snake does with its head and tail." When the man asked for a detailed explanation, Sun Wu began, "If you hit a snake on its head, the snake counters with its tail. If you hit it on its tail, it strikes back with its head. If you strike its body, it fights back with both its head and tail. Therefore, a competent general must arrange his army in a 'Snake Formation' so that it fights like an integrated whole that can protect the front, the middle, and the rear at the same time. Only then can the army hold itself together instead of being routed."

The man still didn't seem to fully understand, for he pressed for more clarification, saying, "How can you guarantee that the officers and men in such a 'Snake Formation' will be well coordinated as an integrated whole?"

"There's no need to worry," said Sun Wu. "A battleground is a place of life and death. Wars force an army to fight like one man."

Seeing that the man was still puzzled, Sun Wu patiently told him an incident that he had experienced. "You know that the states of Wu and Yue have been constantly at war, and the people of the two states hate each other as sworn enemies. One day, travelers from both states happened to cross a river on the same ferry. At first, they glared at each other with great animosity, ready to fight at any moment. But when the boat was halfway across the river, a storm sprang up and kicked up wave after wave, threatening to capsize the ferry. To live, the travelers had to set aside their enmity and work together to balance the ferry. Eventually, they survived the storm and arrived at the other side of the river safe and sound."

After a brief pause, Sun Wu added meaningfully, "On the verge of a grave danger, even enemies can sail on the same boat, not to mention the officers and men in a 'Snake Formation' who bear no grudges against one another and are as close as brothers. They're bound to fight together like a snake, taking care of both the front and the rear and coming to each other's rescue." The man felt Sun Wu's remarks made a great deal of sense.

This proverb is a metaphor that illustrates how people, whether bearing grudges against or sharing common interests with each other, can work together to overcome a common difficulty.

# 同舟共济

这条成语出自《孙子·九地》，作者孙武（前544－前496）是中国春秋时期著名军事家，被后人尊称为孙子。

一天，有人问孙武怎样布阵才能不被敌人击败。孙武回答说："用兵<u>布阵</u>应该像蛇<u>反击</u>猎手一样，蛇形阵能够首尾<u>兼顾</u>成为一个整体。"那人请孙武说得再<u>详细</u>一些。于是孙武便<u>解释</u>起来了："打蛇的时候，你如果打它的头部，它会用尾巴反击你；你去打它的尾巴，它又会用头部来<u>袭击</u>你；你如果打它的腰部，它就用头尾一齐来<u>夹击</u>你。所以，善于布阵的将领也要将军队摆成蛇一样的<u>阵势</u>，使全军形成一个整体，能够前、中、后彼此<u>照应</u>。只有这样才不会被敌人<u>击溃</u>"。

那人显然没有完全明白孙武的意思，<u>追问</u>道："怎么见得将士们会在蛇阵里相互配合成一个整体呢？"

孙武说："这个不必担心，战场乃生死之地，战争会迫使军队齐心协力的。"孙武见那人还是有些<u>疑惑</u>不解的样子，就<u>耐心</u>地给他讲了一个亲身经历的故事："你知道，吴国和越国之间经常打仗，两国人民也都将对方视为仇人。有一次，来自两国的人要渡河，<u>恰巧</u>坐在了一条船上。船刚开的时候，他们相互<u>怒视</u>着，一副要打架的样子。但当船开到河中央的时候，突然风雨大作，波涛滚滚，眼见船就要翻了，为了保住性命，他们顾不得彼此的仇恨，合力稳住船身，终于战胜风浪，安全到达河的对岸。"孙武顿了顿，<u>意味深长</u>地说："大难临头之际，连仇人都能同舟共济，更何况蛇阵里那些没冤没仇，兄弟情深的将士们呢？他们必然会像蛇一样成为一个整体，首尾相顾，彼此救援。"那人觉得孙武说得非常有道理。

这条成语比喻，即使存在<u>分歧</u>的人们，只要团结互助、<u>齐心协力</u>，也能战胜共同的困难，更何况<u>志同道合</u>的人们呢。

## Vocabulary

| Characters | Pinyin | Word Type | Translation |
| --- | --- | --- | --- |
| 布阵 | bùzhèn | V. | to deploy troops for battle |
| 兼顾 | jiāngù | V. | to attend to multiple things at once, to balance (career, family, kids, etc.) |
| 详细 | xiángxì | ADJ. | specific |
| 解释 | jiěshì | V. | to explain |
| 袭击 | xíjī | V./N. | to attack; attack |
| 夹击 | jiājī | V. | to attack from both sides |
| 阵势 | zhènshì | N. | battle array, situation |
| 照应 | zhàoyìng | V. | to coordinate |
| 击溃 | jīkuì | V. | to rout, to put to flight |
| 追问 | zhuīwèn | V. | to question closely |
| 疑惑不解 | yíhuò bùjiě | V. | to doubt, to be puzzled |
| 耐心 | nàixīn | ADJ./ADV. | patient; patiently |
| 恰巧 | qiàqiǎo | ADV. | by chance, as it happens |
| 怒视 | nùshì | V. | to glare |
| 意味深长 | yìwèi shēncháng | EXPR. | profound, significant, meaningful |
| 分歧 | fēnqí | N. | difference, ramification |
| 齐心合力 | qíxīn hélì | EXPR. | to make concerted efforts |
| 志同道合 | zhì tóng dào hé | EXPR. | to have a common goal; like-minded |

## Examples

中美两国之间虽存在不少分歧，但在威胁全人类的挑战面前，还是应该<u>同舟共济</u>。

Despite their differences, the United States and China can still **work together on the same boat** to fight challenges that face humanity at large.

那场比赛打得十分艰难，多亏所有球员<u>同舟共济</u>，奋勇拼搏，才最终赢得了胜利。

It was a tough tournament, but playing bravely together **as if on the same boat in a tempest**, the players eventually came out as the winner.

# Sleeping on Sticks and Eating Bile

| 卧 | 薪 | 尝 | 胆 |
|---|---|---|---|
| wò | xīn | cháng | dǎn |
| to lie | fuel, fire wood | to taste, to try | gall bladder, gall |

**Literal translation:** Lie on firewood and taste gall.

**Meaning:** Enduring hardships, especially self-imposed ones, to build the resolve to accomplish something ambitious.

This proverb comes from the *Records of the Grand Historian* by Sima Qian (c. 145–86 BCE), a historian of the Han dynasty (206 BCE–220 CE). He is considered the father of Chinese historiography.

# Sleeping on Sticks and Eating Bile

In 494 BCE, King Fu Chai of the State of Wu launched an attack against the State of Yue to avenge his father, who had been killed by King Gou Jian of Yue in a previous battle. After defeating his army, King Fu Chai captured King Gou Jian. Instead of killing him, King Fu Chai decided to subject his captive to a life of humiliation by making him his horse keeper.

Gou Jian acted as if he had been unbothered and put on a show of resignation. In his mind, however, he never gave up the hope of recovering his lost state. Pretending to be submissive, he used every means to gain King Fu Chai's trust. He even went so far as to taste the king's stool to tell about his physical condition. Acts like this effectively diminished King Fu Chai's vigilance, making him believe that Gou Jian had completely lost his will to fight. The smart prime minister of the State of Wu, however, did not think that was the case. He saw through Gou Jian's intention, but his advice fell on deaf ears. The willful King Fu Chai even released Gou Jian and allowed him to return to his Yue territory.

Back from his bondage in the State of Wu, King Gou Jian had nothing on his mind but the recovery of his state and revenge against his captor and humiliator. Nevertheless, Yue was still weak in every aspect. Gou Jian had no alternative but to lie low and do everything he could to renew the state's economic and military strength. Doing so, as he knew, would take several years. In order not to forget the hardships he had suffered at the hands of his foe and not to lose his resolve to fight, he divorced himself from the extravagant life of a king. Instead, he had his comfortable bed replaced with a mattress of sticks and twigs. He also hung a hog's gallbladder above his dinner table so that he could eat a bit of the bile before each meal—for the Chinese speak of enduring hardships as "eating bitterness."

While rebuilding the state of Yue, King Gou Jian managed to weaken the state of Wu by using a beautiful woman named Xi Shi to seduce King Fu Chai and alienate him from his smart prime minister. Eventually, King Gou Jian felt Yue was strong enough. Together with the allied State of Qi, the army of Yue routed King Fu Chai's troops. Right before King Gou Jian could get hold of him, King Fu Chai committed suicide.

This proverb encourages people to endure self-imposed hardships to cultivate their resolve and fortitude to do something big.

# 卧薪尝胆

这条成语源自司马迁的《史记》。司马迁是中国汉代(公元前206年－公元220年)的史官，被后人尊为中国历史编纂的鼻祖。

公元前494年，吴王夫差为报杀父之仇，对越国发起了进攻，最终<u>打败</u>了越王勾践，将其俘获。吴王不想杀死越王，而是让做他的马夫，以此来<u>羞辱</u>他，让他生不如死。

勾践似乎并不在意，默默地接受了这一角色。而实际上，他复国的希望从未<u>泯灭</u>。他以表面绝对服从，来换取夫差对他的信任。为此，夫差患病时，勾践不惜他的粪便放到嘴里去尝，据此来判断他的病情。诸如此类的做法，让夫差对勾践完全放松了<u>警惕</u>，认为他再也没有了反抗的意志。然而，睿智的吴国宰相并不这么想，他已经看出了勾践的盘算。不幸的是，夫差把他的忠告当作<u>耳旁风</u>，居然<u>放虎归山</u>，让勾践回到越的<u>故土</u>。

逃脱吴王夫差的魔掌回到越国，越王勾践满脑子都是复国和复仇的念头，他要<u>一雪胯下之辱</u>。但问题是，残破的越国<u>积贫积弱</u>；为了集中精力发展经济和军事实力，他不得不<u>隐忍</u>。然而，要让越国强大起来，岂能<u>一蹴而就</u>。为了能够在几年间、甚至十几年间都不会忘记吴王夫差强加给他的屈辱，也为了避免斗志被日益消磨，越王勾践决心不再继续享受过去的奢华生活。他每天就睡在薪柴铺成的床垫上，吃饭前总要尝一口悬挂在饭桌上方的猪苦胆。中国人把经受艰苦的磨练比喻作"吃苦"。

越王勾践一边重建自己的王国，一边用美人计和离间计来削弱吴国的国力。终于有一天，勾践觉得他的国力已经足够强大，于是联合<u>盟邦</u>齐国，击溃了吴国的军队，吴王夫差在越王勾践逮到他之前便自杀了。

这条成语，鼓励人们要通过吃苦来增强自己的<u>韧性</u>，唯有如此，才能做成大事。

## Vocabulary

| Characters | Pinyin | Word Type | Translation |
| --- | --- | --- | --- |
| 打败 | dǎbài | V. | to defeat |
| 羞辱 | xiūrǔ | V. | to shame |
| 泯灭 | mǐnmiè | V. | to disappear, to obliterate |
| 警惕 | jǐngtì | V. | to be alert, to warn |
| 睿智 | ruìzhì | ADJ. | intelligent, wise |
| 耳旁风 | ěr páng fēng | N. | advice that is ignored (lit., wind beside one's ear) |
| 放虎归山 | fàng hǔ guī shān | EXPR. | lit. set a tiger free and let it return to its mountain, a metaphor for creating a future calamity |
| 故土 | gùtǔ | N. | homeland, native land |
| 隐忍 | yǐnrěn | V. | to bear with, to endure |
| 一蹴而就 | yī cù ér jiù | V. | to achieve something with one move, to get results overnight |
| 盟邦 | méngbāng | N. | ally |
| 韧性 | rènxìng | N. | tenacity |

## Examples

中国足球队需要发挥卧薪尝胆的精神，刻苦训练，才能冲出亚洲。

The Chinese soccer team needs to train hard with the spirit of Gou Jian, **who inflicted hardships on himself to bolster his resolve**, before it can win championships in Asia and compete in the world arena.

我女儿并没有因为今年高考失利而气馁，她说她要卧薪尝胆，努力复习，明年再战。

Undaunted by her failure in this year's college entrance examinations, my daughter has vowed to study hard for next year's exam, **enduring any hardships that might arise in the process.**

# Killing Two Birds with One Arrow

| 一 | 箭 | 双 | 雕 |
|---|---|---|---|
| *yī* | *jiàn* | *shuāng* | *diāo* |
| one | arrow | pair, double | vulture, bird of prey |

**Literal translation:** One arrow, two vultures.

**Meaning:** Accomplishing two goals with one action.

**English equivalent:** Killing two birds with one stone.

The story that gave birth to this proverb was first recorded in the *History of the Northern Dynasties*, which covers the period from 386 to 618 CE. Another version of the story can be found in the *Book of the New Tang*, compiled by Ouyang Xiu (1007–1072) and others in the Song dynasty. Both are part of the famous multi-volume history classic *Twenty-Four Histories of China*.

## Killing Two Birds with One Arrow

According to the story in *The History of the Northern Dynasties*, there was a general named Zhangsun Cheng in the State of Northern Zhou during the Southern and Northern Dynasties (420–589 CE). He was a well-known strategist and an expert archer. When She Tu, the chieftain of the Turkic tribe known as Tujue, came to pick up a daughter of the king of Zhou to honor a previously arranged marriage alliance, the king asked Zhangsun Cheng to escort his daughter to the chieftain's homeland.

One day, when She Tu and Zhangsun Cheng were hunting, two vultures flew into sight. She Tu asked Zhangsun Cheng if he could shoot the birds down. Not only could Zhangsun Cheng do so, but he hit both vultures with one arrow, demonstrating his supreme archery skills.

This proverb is a metaphoric way of saying accomplishing two goals with one action.

# 一箭双雕

这则成语首见于《北史》中记载的一个故事,该书记载了中国公元386至618年之间的历史。另外一个类似的故事见于宋人欧阳修(1007-1072)等人撰写的《新唐书》。《北史》和《新唐书》都是多部头的著名中国历史典籍《二十四史》中的一部分。

《北史》中的故事讲到,南北朝(公元420-589年)的北周有个<u>将军</u>,叫长孙晟。他不仅<u>有智有谋</u>,还<u>善于射箭</u>。这年,突厥国王摄图来到北周,按照<u>事先说定</u>的合婚安排,准备接走北周的一个公主。北周国王便让长孙晟护送公主到突厥。

一天,摄图和长孙晟在一起<u>打猎</u>,眼见飞来两只雕。摄图问长孙晟能否把雕射下来。长孙晟一箭射出,竟然同时射中了那两只雕,一展<u>精湛</u>的箭术。

这则成语用比喻的形式告诉人们:做一件事是可以<u>事半功倍</u>的。

## Vocabulary

| Characters | Pinyin | Word Type | Translation |
|---|---|---|---|
| 将军 | jiāngjūn | N. | general (of an army) |
| 弓箭 | gōng jiàn | N. | bow and arrow |
| 火箭 | huǒ jiàn | N. | rocket |
| 有智有谋 | yǒu zhì yǒu móu | EXPR. | intelligent and resourceful |
| 善于 | shànyú | V. | to be good at |
| 射箭 | shèjiàn | N. | archery |
| 事先 | shìxiān | ADJ. | in advance, beforehand, prior |
| 打猎 | dǎliè | V. | to hunt |
| 精湛 | jīngzhàn | ADJ. | exquisite |
| 事半功倍 | shì bàn gōng bèi | EXPR. | to get twice the result with half the effort, efficient, effective |

## Examples

他上次回中国，既开了会又看望了父母和朋友，真是一箭双雕啊。

During his last trip to China **he killed two birds with one stone** by attending a conference and visiting his parents and friends at the same time.

甲：最近你都干什么啦？

乙：我在学习太极拳。

甲：好啊，学好太极拳是一箭双雕的事情，既学到了一种锻炼身体的方法，又掌握了一定的武术技能。

A: What have been doing lately?

B: I have been learning Tai Chi.

A: Great! Learning Tai Chi is something that can **kill two birds with one stone**: you learn to keep fit and master a martial art at the same time.

# The Fisherman Benefits from the Snipe Grappling with the Clam

| 鹬 | 蚌 | 相 | 争 | 渔翁 | 得 | 利 |
|---|---|---|---|---|---|---|
| yù | bàng | xiāng | zhēng | yú wēng | dé | lì |
| snipe | clam | with (each other) | to struggle, to fight | old fisherman | to achieve | benefit, profit |

**Literal translation:** When the snipe and the clam fight each other, the old fisherman reaps the benefit.

**Meaning:** A dispute between two parties may only benefit a third party.

**English equivalent:** Two dogs fight for a bone, and a third runs away with it.

During the Warring States Period (476–221 BCE), the State of Zhao was planning to attack the State of Yan. A famous advisor named Su Dai went to King Huiwen of Zhao to dissuade him from attacking. To avoid offending the king, Su Dai did his job circuitously: he told the king an allegory. This allegory was later recorded in the renowned ancient Chinese historical text *Strategies of the Warring States*, compiled between the third and the first centuries BCE.

鹬蚌相争，渔翁得利

## The Fisherman Benefits from the Snipe Grappling with the Clam

Su Dai began, "One day, a clam was sunning itself on a river beach with its shell open when a snipe landed and stuck its beak into the open shell trying to snatch the meat. The clam, startled and in pain, slammed its shell closed, pinching the snipe's beak between the two halves. Neither the snipe nor the clam would let go of the other. Stumbling upon the two creatures locked in a stalemate, an old fisherman picked them up, took them home, and cooked them into a delicious meal."

After he finished, Su Dai said to King Huiwen, "If you attack the state of Yan, neither of you would be able to defeat the other, and you both would be weakened in the stalemate. I am afraid that the powerful Qin would then, acting like the old fisherman, take advantage of the situation and annex both the states of Zhao and Yan. I really hope you will reconsider your decision." Upon the advisor's words, King Huiwen of Zhao withdrew his plan to attack Yan.

This proverb admonishes us to think twice before getting into a dispute, lest we only hurt ourselves in the process while a third party benefits from our weakened position.

# 鹬蚌相争，渔翁得利

战国时期（公元前476‐221年），赵国准备攻打燕国。战国著名的谋士苏代去游说赵惠王，劝说他不要<u>采取行动</u>。为避免<u>惹恼</u>惠王，苏代采取了一个<u>迂回</u>的策略，先给惠王讲了一个寓言。该寓言收录在中国古代名著《战国策》中。《战国策》的成书时间在公元前三世纪至一世纪之间。

苏代开始讲他的寓言故事，"有一天，一只河蚌张开它的<u>贝壳</u>，在河边的沙滩上晒太阳。忽然飞来一只鹬鸟，把它的长<u>喙</u>径直插进河蚌张开的嘴巴里，想要<u>啄</u>出里边的肉饱餐一顿。惊吓和疼痛让河蚌猛地把壳子闭合起来，紧紧地夹住了鹬鸟的长喙。鹬鸟和河蚌互不松口。就在此时，来了一个渔翁，于是就把<u>争持</u>不下的它们一起捡回了家，做成一顿美餐。"

苏代讲完故事，便对惠文王说道，"您去攻打燕国，谁也没有办法把对方打败，却在对峙的过程中<u>削弱</u>了<u>彼此</u>。我担心，强大的秦国就会像渔翁一样从中得利，<u>吞并</u>赵燕两国。我真地希望，<u>陛下</u>能够重新考虑已经做出的决定。"听了策士苏代的话后，赵惠王便<u>撤销</u>了攻打燕国的计划。

这则成语告诫我们，在卷入某个争议之前要<u>三思而行</u>，以免在我们双双受到伤害以后，让他人从我们的争议中受益。

## Vocabulary

| Characters | Pinyin | Word Type | Translation |
|---|---|---|---|
| 采取行动 | cǎiqǔ xíngdòng | EXPR. | to take action, to put a policy into action |
| 惹恼 | rěnǎo | V. | to offend |
| 迂回 | yūhuí | ADJ. | indirect, roundabout |
| 贝壳 (贝乔) | bèiké (bèiqiào) | N. | shell |
| 喙 | huì | N. | beak, snout |
| 啄 | zhuó | V. | to peck |
| 争持 | zhēngchí | V. | to refuse to give in |
| 对峙 | duìzhì | N./V. | confrontation/ to confront |
| 削弱 | xuēruò | V. | to weaken, to cripple |
| 彼此 | bǐcǐ | PN. | each other |
| 吞并 | tūnbìng | V. | to annex, to take over |
| 陛下 | bìxià | PN. | your majesty (polite form to address a ruler) |
| 撤销 | chèxiāo | V. | to revoke, to take back, to undo (on a computer) |
| 三思而行 | sān sī ér xíng | EXPR. | lit. think three times before going; fig. think twice before you jump |

## Examples

面对日本侵略者，处于内战中的国共两党认识到，<u>鹬蚌相争，渔翁得利</u>，因此建立了抗日的统一战线。

Faced with the Japanese invaders, both the Nationalists and the Communists realized that continuing their civil war would only benefit the Japanese; therefore, they formed an Anti-Japanese United Front.

两个公司进行旷日持久的缠讼，其结果是<u>鹬蚌相争，渔翁得利</u>，让它们的共同竞争对手取得优势。

The two companies, involved in a prolonged lawsuit against each other **like two dogs fighting for a bone**, will eventually benefit their common competitors.

# Advanced Proverbs

# Using a Picture to Find a Horse

| 按 | 图 | 索 | 骥 |
|---|---|---|---|
| àn | tú | suǒ | jì |
| according to | picture | to look for, to search | lit. a thoroughbred horse; fig. a cultured person, a person of virtue |

**Literal translation:** Finding a thorough-bred horse according to an illustration.

**Meaning:** Acting without flexibility or following a rigid routine; following clues to find something.

This proverb first appeared in a chapter of the *Book of Han* authored by Ban Gu (32–92 CE), a historian of the Eastern Han dynasty. Some scholars, however, attribute the proverb's origin to the essay *Obscure Allusions Used by the Art Circles* written by Yang Shen (1488–1559), a scholar of the Ming dynasty best known for his poetry.

## Using a Picture to Find a Horse

Sun Yang was a horse expert of the state of Qin during the Spring and Autumn period (770–476 BCE). He could tell at a glance whether a horse was of good or bad quality. Therefore, he was often invited to help others judge and select horses. His talent won him the nickname Bo Le, the name of a celestial body believed to oversee the heavenly horses.

One day, Bo Le was traveling when an old horse drawing a cart loaded with salt started neighing at him. Bo Le stopped to approach the horse, only to find it a pedigree with extreme stamina: it could gallop a few hundred miles without a break when he had been young. Watching the horse trudging quietly away with great difficulty, Sun Yang was sad and could not help shedding tears. He felt that the horse had been mistreated and misused. It could have gone all out galloping across battlegrounds instead of having its talent and prowess wasted on working as a beast of burden.

Bo Le decided to teach people how to tell good horses from inferior ones so that they could avoid stifling the aptitude of those able to gallop a few hundred miles without a break. To achieve this goal, he wrote a book with text and illustrations to shed light on the characteristics and appearances of various kinds of horses. He based the book on the knowledge he had accumulated over the years and named it *A Classic on Distinguishing Horses*.

One of Bo Le's young sons read the book and thought it easy to tell good horses from inferior ones. He cast about for good horses according to the pictures and descriptions in the book. Unable to find one bearing the exact resemblance to any of the illustrated horses, he turned to the captions only. Eventually, he found a toad that he thought fitted a textual description of a good horse. With great joy, he brought the toad home and showed it to his father, saying, "Dad! I've finally found a great horse, only it has mediocre hooves." Seeing the toad, Bo Le didn't know whether to laugh or cry. He had not expected that his son would have been so dumb. But a father is a father, and he said with good humor, "Unfortunately, your horse likes to jump too much, and you can't use it to draw a cart." Then he sighed and said to himself, "This is an extreme example of depending too much on an illustration to find a horse."

The proverb was used originally to express the idea that we shouldn't be bound by old conventions at the expense of flexibility and original thinking. Today, however, it has the extended meaning of looking for something by following clues.

# 按图索骥

这条成语最早出自东汉班固（公元32-92年）的《汉书·梅福传》。也有人认为出自明朝杨慎（1488-1559年）的《艺林伐山》。

  春秋时候，秦国有个叫孙阳的人，<u>擅长</u>相马，无论什么样的马，他一眼就能<u>分出优劣</u>。他常常被人请去识马、选马，人们都称他为"伯乐"。"伯乐"本来是天上一颗星星的名字，据说是负责管理天马的。

  有一次，伯乐路过一个地方，忽见一匹拖着盐车的马冲他嘶鸣个不停，走近一看，原来<u>匹千里马</u>，只是年龄稍大了点。老马拉着车艰难地走着，孙阳觉得太委屈了这匹千里马，它本是可以奔跑于疆场、发挥更大作用的<u>宝马良驹</u>，现在却<u>默默无闻</u>地拖着盐车，慢慢地消耗着它的锐气和体力，实在可惜！孙阳想到这里，难过得落下泪来。

  为了让更多的人学会相马，使千里马不再被<u>埋没</u>，伯乐就把自己多年<u>积累</u>的经验和知识写成一本书，配上各种马的形态图，书名叫《相马经》。

  伯乐有个儿子，看了父亲写的《相马经》，以为相马很容易，就拿着这本书到处找好马。他按照书上所绘的图形去找，<u>一无所获</u>。又按书中所写的特征去找，最后发现有一只<u>癞蛤蟆</u>很像书中写的千里马，便高兴地把癞蛤蟆带回家，对父亲说："爸爸，我找到一匹千里马，只是蹄子稍差些。"父亲一看，哭笑不得，没想到儿子竟如此愚笨，便幽默地说："可惜这马太喜欢跳了，不能用来拉车。" 接着感叹道："所谓按图索骥也。"

  成语"按图索骥"，比喻<u>机械</u>地照老办法做事，不知道变通；现在，也比喻按照某种线索去寻找事。

## Vocabulary

| Characters | Pinyin | Word Type | Translation |
|---|---|---|---|
| 擅长 | shàncháng | V. | to be good at |
| 优劣 | yōuliè | ADJ. | good or bad, good from bad |
| 千里马 | qiānlǐmǎ | N. | a horse with great stamina |
| 宝马良驹 | bǎo mǎ liáng jū | N. | a good horse |
| 默默无闻 | mò mò wú wén | ADJ. | to be buried in oblivion, to be unknown |
| 埋没 | máimò | V. | to stifle, to neglect |
| 积累 | jīlěi | V. | to accumulate |
| 一无所获 | yī wú suǒ huò | EXPR. | to have gained nothing; in vain |
| 癞蛤蟆 | làihámá | N. | toad |
| 机械 | jīxiè | ADV. | mechanically, rigidly |
| 效率 | xiàolǜ | N. | efficiency |

## Examples

他做什么事情都是<u>按图索骥</u>，效率太低。

He sticks to rigid routine for everything he does, which makes him extremely inefficient.

甲：我的智能手机落在厕所被人拿走，不久又失而复得。

乙：真的？怎么回事？

甲：我把卫星追踪图打印下来交给警察，他们<u>按图索骥</u>，帮我找了回来。

A: I had left my smart phone in the bathroom and it had been taken by someone. But soon I got it back.

B: Really? How?

A: I printed out the GPS tracking map, and with it the police officers managed to retrieve my phone.

# Seeing a Horse Whizzing by Through a Crack in the Wall

| 白 | 驹 | 过 | 隙 |
|---|---|---|---|
| *bái* | *jū* | *guò* | *xì* |
| white | steed | to pass | crack, crevice |

**Literal translation:** A white steed passes a crack in the wall.

**Meaning:** Life is short; time flies.

This proverb originates from a section of the classic *Zhuangzi*, describing a conversation between the philosophers Confucius and Laozi. The *Zhuangzi* is attributed to the eponymous philosopher Zhuangzi, active as the central figure of Daoism during the Warring States period (475–221 BCE). It contains stories and anecdotes expounding on the Daoist ideal of being carefree. A later classic, the *Book of Rites*, mentions a slightly different version of this proverb, quoting Confucius as saying, "four passing horses seen through a crack in a wall." Although different from the single white horse mentioned in the Zhuangzi version, the two sayings have the same meaning.

## Seeing a Horse Whizzing by Through a Crack in the Wall

According to the philosopher Zhuangzi, Confucius paid a special visit to Laozi to learn more about the latter's philosophy. The two greeted each other and sat down on a mat spread out on the floor as chairs were unknown until a later time. After some small talk, Confucius initiated the conversation between the two greatest minds in the recorded history of China.

"The profoundness of your knowledge is so impressive that I've come to see you as I'm not busy today," said Confucius. "Could you please tell me something about your Daoist philosophy?"

"The philosophy of Daoism," said Laozi, "is so esoteric and mysterious that it's beyond words. But since you're so humble as to come and ask me, let me give it a try."

Laozi started his lengthy discourse. While talking about the ephemerality of life, he used a metaphor with a big sigh, "Human life is short, and time goes by as quickly as a passing white steed that we see through a crack in a wall."

Laozi's reference to the transience of life was so vivid that it soon became widely known and has since been a synonym for "time flies" among learned Chinese.

# 白驹过隙

这条成语出自《庄子·外篇·知北游》。该书作者与书同名，是战国时期（公元前475–221年）道家学派的代表人物。《庄子》通过很多故事和<u>轶事</u>，阐述了"无为"这一道家学派认为人们应该到达的<u>理想境界</u>。

《礼记》似乎印证了《庄子》故事中有关孔子和老子的会面，正是在他们的这次交谈中产生了"白驹过隙"这则成语，尽管《礼记》引用孔子的话，说的是"若驷之过隙"，（"驷"指的是套在车上的四匹马，与"白驹过隙"中的为少壮骏马的"驹"稍有不同），但两种说法的意思完全相同。

据《庄子》<u>记载</u>，孔子专程去拜访老子，向他请教其道学的学问。他们互致了问候，便席地而坐（其时椅子尚未在中国出现）。<u>稍事寒暄</u>之后，中国有史以来两个最伟大的思想家便开始了<u>空前绝后</u>的对话。

孔子对老子说，"先生学问高深，<u>趁今天有空</u>，我前来拜访，请你给我讲一讲你的道学。"

"道的学问，既<u>深奥</u>又<u>玄妙</u>，很难用言语来表达啊。先生既然<u>不耻下问</u>，那我还是试着说一说吧。"老子于是就<u>滔滔不绝</u>地阐述起他的道学思想来。<u>说着说着</u>，便讲到了人生苦短的问题。老子不禁感叹道，"短得就象透过墙的<u>缝隙</u>观看外边飞驰而过的白马，眨眼间就过去了。"

<u>由于</u>"白驹过隙"的说法形象生动，后来，有点儿学问的人们就开始用这个成语来表示"时间过得飞快"的意思了。

## Vocabulary

| Characters | Pinyin | Word Type | Translation |
|---|---|---|---|
| 轶事 | yìshì | N. | anecdote |
| 理想境界 | lǐxiǎng jìng jiè | N. | ideal |
| 编撰 | biānzhuàn | V. | to compile |
| 记载 | jìzǎi | V. | to record |
| 稍事 | shāoshì | N. | little things, small matters |
| 寒暄 | hánxuān | V. | to make small talk (to talk about the weather) |
| 空前绝后 | kōng qián jué hòu | EXPR. | unprecedented, unique |
| 趁 | chèn | V. | to take advantage of |
| 深奥 | shēn'ào | ADJ. | profound |
| 玄妙 | xuánmiào | ADJ. | mysterious, profound |
| 不耻下问 | bù chǐ xià wèn | EXPR. | not being ashamed to ask and learn from your subordinates |
| 滔滔不绝 | tāo tāo bù jué | EXPR. / ADV. | talk non-stop |
| 说着说着 | shuō zhe shuō zhe | ADV. | while talking, in the middle of one's talk |
| 缝隙 | fèngxì | N. | crack |
| 由于 | yóuyú | ADV. | because of, due to |

## Examples

时间犹如<u>白驹过隙</u>，在你们这个大家庭中，我已经生活了一年半多了。

**Time flies**. I have lived among your big family for over a year and a half already.

因为人生如<u>白驹过隙</u>般短暂，所以我们要珍惜生命、珍惜时间。

Because **life is short**, we must cherish it and make full use of our time.

# Eight Immortals Crossing the Sea, Flaunting Their Magic Power

| 八 | 仙 | 过 | 海 | 各 | 显 | 其 | 能 |
|---|---|---|---|---|---|---|---|
| bā | xiān | guò | hǎi | gè | xiǎn | qí | néng |
| eight | immortals | to cross, to pass | sea, ocean | each, every | to demonstrate | his, her, its | capability, to be able to |

**Meaning:** Each person has a unique way of solving a problem; every participant in a contest vying with one another to win.

The Daoist concept of *baxian*, or the Eight Immortals, first emerged in the Tang (618–907 CE) and Song (960–1279) dynasties, although who exactly make up the group differs in different stories. The assemblage of immortals mentioned in the following story was initially described in *Journey to the East*, a novel by Daoist writer Wu Yuantai of the Ming dynasty (1368–1644). It was Wu Cheng'en (1501–1582), however, who gave rise to this eight-character proverb in his famous novel *Journey to the West*.

# Eight Immortals Crossing the Sea, Flaunting Their Magic Power

The Eight Immortals were ordinary men and women who later acquired their godly status. The most accepted group of Eight Immortals consists of Tieguai Li, Zhongli Quan, Zhang Guolao, Lü Dongbin, He Xiangu, Lan Caihe, Han Xiangzi, and Cao Guojiu. Tieguai Li limped with his hallmark iron crutch. His handicap was the result of a mistake by his disciples, who had burned his physical body while his spirit was traveling elsewhere. When the spirit had returned, it had had nowhere to reside but the dead body of a lame beggar. Zhongli Quan had been a general. After a lost battle, he had been introduced to an immortal, who had taught him to become an immortal himself. Zhang Guolao had used to be a magician. After becoming an immortal, he got into the habit of riding a white donkey backwards. When he wasn't riding, he would fold the beast up like a piece of paper and place it in a leather pouch. Lü Dongbin had turned into an immortal after he met first Zhongli Quan and then the Fiery Dragon God. Later, after he learned swordsmanship from another immortal, he became the champion of the weak. The only female of the group, He Xiangu, was good at telling fortunes. Lan Caihe was known for his never-aging face. Han Xiangzi had been an alcoholic dandy. Cao Guojiu, a brother-in-law of an emperor, had used to be very powerful and wicked. After narrowly escaping execution for his misdeeds, this pardoned man transformed into an immortal.

Each year, the Queen Mother of the West, the Goddess of Life and Death, would invite all deities to her party on the Kunlun Mountains. Leaving the banquet, the intoxicated Eight Immortals decided to go on an adventure, that is, a race across the East Sea with the help of their magical apparatuses. They wanted to see whose was the most powerful and effective. Tieguai Li cast his crutch into the water and sailed on it as if it were a boat; Zhongli Quan floated on his horsetail whisk; Zhang Guolao waded on his donkey; Lü Dongbin, on his vertical bamboo flute; Han Xiangzi, on his flower basket; He Xiangu, on her lotus leaf; Lan Caihe, on his clappers; and Cao Guojiu, on his jade tablet.

Halfway across the water, they ran into the oldest son of the Dragon King of the East Sea. In their encounter, the prince managed to take possession of Lan Caihe's jade clappers. The dragon prince's refusal to return the clappers led to a fight and his death. To avenge his son's death, the bereaved Dragon King launched an attack against the Eight Immortals. In their rage, the immortals dried up the East Sea with a fire released from their magical gourds and took over the Dragon King's palace. The humiliated Dragon King fled and later returned with his brothers, the Dragon Kings of the West, South, and North Seas. They and their marine armies fought the Eight Immortals together and recovered the palace. The vexed immortals then toppled Mount Tai by the East Sea, trying to fill up the sea with its debris. Vowing to retaliate, the Dragon Kings lodged a complaint with the Jade Emperor of Heaven, who dispatched a celestial army to suppress the immortals.

The battle raged on for days before Guanyin, the Buddhist Goddess of Mercy, intervened on behalf of the Buddha and Laozi. The Eight Immortals apologized and resumed their journey east while Guanyin restored Mount Tai and the East Sea to their original state. The Dragon Kings eventually retired to their respective marine palaces.

This proverb has two morals: one tells us that each member of a team has a unique strength that he or she can contribute; the other describes a situation where participants in a contest or competition each are trying their best to win.

# 八仙过海，各显其能

作为道教神祇的"八仙"最早出现于唐（618-907）宋（960-1279）时期，但是八仙中的人物并不固定。现在为人所知的八仙是由明代信奉道教的作家吴元泰在其《八仙出东游记》（也叫《东游记》）一书中固定下来的，而这条八字成语则出于吴承恩（1501-1582）的名著《西游记》。

八仙成仙之前都是<u>凡夫俗子</u>。现在被大家熟知并认可的八仙有：铁拐李、钟离权、张果老、吕洞宾、何仙姑、蓝采和、韩湘子和曹国舅。铁拐李以其跛脚和铁拐而得名。他的残疾要<u>归罪</u>于他的徒弟们：一次，他灵魂出窍外出远游，而他的徒弟们以为他已经亡故，于是就把他的肉身给烧掉了。灵魂回来时发现已无处附着，于是就附体在一个死去的跛脚乞丐的肉身上。钟离权曾经是位将军，一次作战失利，有人便介绍他认识了一个仙人，在其教化下成仙。张果老本是<u>魔术师</u>出身，成仙后，养成一个倒骑驴的习惯。他的白毛驴子不用的时候，可以像纸一样<u>折叠</u>起来放进皮袋子中。吕洞宾是遇到钟离权和火龙真君后得道成仙的，后来又从另一位仙人那里学到了剑术，成了<u>除暴安良</u>的英雄。何仙姑是八仙中唯一一位女性，善于<u>占卜</u>；蓝采和因其永不衰老的娃娃脸而著称；韩湘子则是一个<u>玩世不恭</u>的酒徒。曹国舅本是权重一时的皇亲国戚，但因<u>恶贯满盈</u>，险遭枭首。赦免后<u>痛改前非</u>而成仙。

八仙参加了掌管生死大权的女神西王母的宴会，各个都喝得醉醺醺的。于是他们想进行一次冒险，比试一下，看谁的神器能够抢先把他渡过东海。铁拐李把他的铁拐丢进海里，像船一样坐了上去；钟离权也<u>不甘示弱</u>地坐上他的马尾拂子；张果老骑上他的驴子；吕洞宾则乘上他的竹箫；韩湘子稳坐在他的篮子里；何仙姑盘坐在她的荷叶上；蓝采和脚踏他的大拍板；曹国舅也把他的玉板当作舟船。

他们在海上行至半路，遭遇了东海龙王的儿子。<u>骄横</u>的王子把蓝采和的大拍板偷了去拒不返还。在一番争斗中，八仙杀了他。悲痛欲绝的东海龙王誓为儿子报仇，发兵攻打八仙。八仙<u>盛怒</u>之下从宝葫芦里放出神火煮干了海水，占领了龙宫。遭受<u>奇耻大辱</u>的东海龙王，逃到他的兄弟那里搬来救兵。于是他和他的兄弟南海龙王、西海龙王、北海龙王以及他们的虾兵蟹将，<u>齐心合力</u>战胜了八仙，夺回了东海龙宫。八仙<u>火冒三丈</u>，<u>索性</u>把东海边上的泰山<u>掀翻</u>，推入东海欲将其填平。龙王们哪里肯放过八仙，遂跑到玉皇大帝那里去诉苦。玉皇大帝便差遣他的天兵天将下界去镇压八仙。

双方鏖战多日，终被观音叫停。观音是代表佛祖和老子前来干预的。结果，那边八仙道歉后继续上了路，这边观音恢复了泰山和东海的原貌，让龙王们各归其所。

这条成语有两层意思：一是告诉人们，在一个团队共事的时候，每个人都能发挥其特长；另一个意思是，参与竞赛或竞争的人们都会不遗余力地为获胜而努力。

## Vocabulary

| Characters | Pinyin | Word Type | Translation |
|---|---|---|---|
| 凡夫俗子 | fán fū sú zǐ | N. | ordinary people, mortals |
| 归罪 | guīzuì | V. | to blame |
| 魔术师 | móshùshī | N. | magician |
| 折叠 | zhédié | V. | to fold |
| 除暴安良 | chú bào ān liáng | EXPR. | to get rid of the cruel and pacify the good people |
| 占卜 | zhànbǔ | V. | to practice divination |
| 玩世不恭 | wán shì bù gōng | EXPR. | to be cynical |
| 恶贯满盈 | è guàn mǎn yíng | ADJ. | extremely evil |
| 痛改前非 | tòng gǎi qián fēi | EXPR. | to amend one's past misdeeds |
| 不甘示弱 | bù gān shì ruò | EXPR. | reluctant to show weakness; |
| 骄横 | jiāohèng | ADJ. | arrogant |
| 誓 | shì | V./ N. | to vow, swear; oath |
| 报仇 | bàochóu | V. | to revenge, to avenge |
| 盛怒 | shèngnù | N. | wrath |
| 奇耻大辱 | qí chǐ dà rǔ | N. | a burning shame, a great insult |
| 齐心合力 | qí xīn hé lì | V. | to make concerted efforts |
| 火冒三丈 | huǒ mào sān zhàng | V. | to fly into a rage |
| 索性 | suǒxìng | ADV. | might as well, simply |
| 掀翻 | xiānfān | V. | to topple, to overthrow |
| 鏖战 | áozhàn | V. | to fight fiercely |
| 干预 | gānyù | V. | to intervene |
| 恢复 | huīfù | V. | to restore |

## Examples

为参加这场发明创造比赛,参赛的队员们<u>八仙过海,各显其能</u>,充分发挥他们的聪明才智,创制出卓越的参赛产品。

To compete in the innovation contest, members of the team all did their best **and brought their unique talents into full play**, resulting in a superb product for the event.

甲:演唱会大获成功!你和你们班的同学表演得最好!

乙:是呀,我们<u>八仙过海,各显其能</u>。

A: The talent show was a great success. You and your classmates did the best!

B: I agree. **Each of us went all out to demonstrate his or her special skills**.

# No Tiger's Den, No Tiger's Cub

| 不 | 入 | 虎穴 | 焉 | 得 | 虎子 |
|---|---|---|---|---|---|
| bù | rù | hǔxúe | yān | dé | hǔzǐ |
| no, not | to enter | tiger's den | how to…? (archaic) | to obtain | tiger's cubs |

**Literal translation:** Not going into a tiger's den, one is not going to get a tiger cub.

**Meaning:** It is necessary to take a risk.

**English equivalent:** Nothing ventured, nothing gained; no pain, no gain.

This proverb is attributed to two different sources. One is the volume on the state of Wu in the *Records of the Three Kingdoms*, a historical text covering the period 220–265 CE by Chen Shou, a contemporary official and writer. The other is the biography of Ban Chao, an Eastern Han dynasty (25–220 CE) statesman and diplomat, found in the *Book of the Later Han* authored by Fan Ye, a historian from the Former Song (or Liu) dynasty (420–479 CE).

## No Tiger's Den, No Tiger's Cub

One day, Emperor Ming of the Eastern Han dispatched Ban Chao to present-day Xinjiang Province to befriend King Guang of Shanshan, then a kingdom along the Silk Road. Leading an entourage of thirty-six men, Ban Chao trudged onward despite the daunting distance and soaring mountains. After traveling more than a thousand miles, they eventually arrived in Shanshan. King Guang came out of the city to great Ban Chao and his people, treating them as distinguished guests. The king was very happy to learn of Ban Chao's mission to befriend him.

A few days later, an envoy of the Xiongnu, a fierce nomadic tribe, also arrived with a mission to befriend King Guang. The king likewise entertained him and his entourage with great courtesy. The Xiongnu envoy, however, badmouthed the Eastern Han in King Guang's presence, making the king suspicious of Ban Chao's intentions. The next day, King Guang shunned Ban Chao and even had his soldiers keep watch on him and his people. Ban Chao immediately rallied his men up to figure out a countermeasure. Ban Chao said, "The only way to persuade the king to trust us again is to kill the Xiongnu envoy and his men." Someone murmured worriedly, "We only have thirty-some people while they have an army of well-trained and well-equipped soldiers. Besides, their barracks are highly fortified. How are we going to get rid of them?"

Ban Chao asserted, "We can't grab the tiger cubs if we don't take the risk of going into the tiger's den." That night, Ban Chao and his men snuck into the Xiongnu barracks. They split into two forces, one lurking behind the barracks with their battle drums ready, the other lying in ambush on both sides of the barracks with bows and swords poised. They then set fire to the barracks while yelling and beating their drums. The Xiongnu envoy and his troops were thrown into a panic. In the end, all the Xiongnu were either burned or shot to death with bows and arrows.

Learning of the Eastern Han's genuine intention to establish a good relationship with his kingdom, King Guang of Shanshan reconciled with Ban Chao.

Ban Chao's metaphor means we have to take risks if we're to accomplish our goals, after all, "nothing ventured, nothing gained." Today, this proverb is also used to express the necessity of hard work, as in "no pain, no gain."

# 不入虎穴，焉得虎子

这条成语一说出自《三国志·吴书·吕蒙传》。《三国志》是由西晋著名史学家陈寿（233-297）所著，记载中国三国时期的断代史。又一说出自《后汉书·班超传》。班超是东汉著名<u>将领</u>、<u>外交家</u>.《后汉书》是一部由我国宋代南朝时期的历史学家范晔（398-445）编撰的纪传体史书，记载了东汉的历史，与《史记》、《汉书》、《三国志》合称"前四史"。

  东汉时，汉明帝派班超到新疆去，和叫广的鄯善王交朋友。班超带着一行人马三十六人，不怕山高路远，一路跋涉而去。他们<u>千里迢迢</u>，来到了新疆。鄯善王听说班超<u>出使西域</u>，亲自出城迎候。<u>东道主把班超奉为上宾</u>。班超向主人说明来意，鄯善王很高兴。

  过了几天，匈奴也派使者来和鄯善王<u>联络感情</u>。鄯善王热情<u>款</u>待他们。匈奴人在主人面前说了东汉许多坏话，使得鄯善王对班超的来意产生了<u>怀疑</u>。第二天，他拒不接见班超，态度十分冷淡。他甚至派兵<u>监视</u>班超。班超立刻召集大家商量<u>对策</u>。班超说："只有除掉匈奴使者才能消除主人的疑虑，两国和好。"有人担心地说，"可是我们只有三十几个人，而匈奴使者他们却<u>兵强马壮</u>，防守又十分严密，我们怎么能把他们除掉呢？"

  班超说："不入虎穴，焉得虎子！"这天深夜，班超带了士兵潜到匈奴营地。他们兵分两路，一路拿着战鼓躲在营地后面，一路手执弓箭刀枪埋伏在营地两旁。他们一面放火烧<u>帐篷</u>，一面击鼓呐喊。匈奴人大乱，结果全被大火烧死、乱箭射死。

  鄯善王明白真相后，便和班超<u>言归于好</u>。

  班超的比喻意味着，要达致一个目标，就要有一定的冒险精神，没有冒险就没有收获。今天，这个成语也说明了艰苦工作的必要性，也就是说，"没有痛苦，就没有收获"。

## Vocabulary

| Characters | Pinyin | Word Type | Translation |
|---|---|---|---|
| 将领 | jiànglǐng | N. | military leader |
| 外交家 | wàijiāojiā | N. | diplomat |
| 千里迢迢 | qiān lǐ tiáo tiáo | ADJ. | far, far away |
| 出使 | chūshǐ | V. | to be sent on a diplomatic mission |
| 西域 | xīyù | N. | an old name for the area that today include Xinjiang and parts of Central Asia |
| 东道主 | dōngdàozhǔ | N. | host |
| 奉为上宾 | fèng wéi shàng bīn | V | to be treated as an honored guest |
| 联络感情 | lián luò gǎn qíng | V | to make a friendly contact |
| 款待 | kuǎndài | V. | to entertain, to treat cordially |
| 怀疑 | huáiyí | V. | to suspect, to doubt, to distrust |
| 监视 | jiānshì | V. | to keep watch on, to monitor |
| 对策 | duìcè | N. | countermeasure |
| 兵强马壮 | bīng qiáng mǎ zhuàng | ADJ. | (of troops) well-trained and equipped |
| 埋伏 | máifú | V. | to ambush, to lie in wait |
| 帐篷 | zhàngpéng | N. | tent |
| 言归于好 | yán guī yú hǎo | EXPR. | to be reconciled with, to make it up with |

## Examples

甲：这个贩毒集团这么狡猾，怎么这么快就一网打尽啦？
乙：警方派了卧底。
甲：好危险啊！
乙：这叫"<u>不入虎穴，焉得虎子</u>"嘛。

A: This drug cartel has been very cunning. How come it has been taken down so quickly?
B: The police planted an undercover officer among the drug dealers.
A: That is very dangerous!
B: As the saying goes, "**nothing ventured, nothing gained.**"

古人有云："<u>不入虎穴，焉得虎子</u>"。想成大事者，正要有这等勇担风险的气魄。

As the old saying goes, "**No tiger's den, no tiger's cub**." One who aspires to success must have the courage to take risks.

# High Mountains, Flowing Water

| 高 | 山 | 流 | 水 |
|---|---|---|---|
| gāo | shān | liú | shuǐ |
| high | mountain | to flow | water |

**Meaning:** A bosom friend; a piece of truly great music.

This proverb comes from the *Liezi*, a Daoist classic attributed to its namesake Liezi, or Lie Yukou, a Daoist philosopher from the Warring States Period who allegedly lived during the fifth century BCE.

## High Mountains, Flowing Water

Yu Boya was a famous musician of the state of Chu during the Spring and Autumn period (770–476 BCE). He demonstrated great musical talent at an early age and later became a student of a master *qin* player named Cheng Lian. The *qin* is a traditional Chinese stringed instrument of the zither family. Even though he excelled at all the techniques that Master Cheng could teach him, Boya was still unsatisfied, feeling unable to fully express his emotions when he played. Cheng Lian took him to his own master on an island in the East Sea. There, Cheng Lian asked Boya to wait patiently for his master and promised to pick him up when the meeting was over. Days passed, but neither Cheng Lian nor his master showed up.

In his solitude, his companions were none other but the birds singing in the forest. Their songs, against the backdrop of the pounding waves, sounded as melancholy as what Boya was feeling, and it struck a chord in his heart. With a sigh, Boya began to pluck his *qin*, which produced the soul-stirring music he had been seeking all along. In fact, this was just what Master Cheng Lian had planned. Later, people observed that Boya played so well that even horses eating at their troughs would raise their heads and listen. Nevertheless, Boya was still unhappy because he found that few could understand the beautiful music he was now able to play.

One day, Boya was traveling on a riverboat when it began to rain. The boat had to seek shelter at the foot of a mountain. Watching the raindrops beating on the heaving waters of the river, Boya felt the urge to play a tune right there on the boat. He was indulging himself with the emotions in his beautiful music when a string snapped. Boya looked up and accidentally caught sight of a woodsman sitting in the rain on the bank. The man, Zhong Ziqi by name, had been listening so attentively to that he had become oblivious to the rain. Deeply touched, Boya invited Zhong Ziqi onto his boat, where he shared his music with him. As soon as Boya finished a tune that he mentally called "High Mountains", Zhong Ziqi verbally painted a picture of unbroken mountain ranges. Then, Boya had just finished performing another tune that he intended to name "Flowing Waters" when Zhong Ziqi told him he had visualized the torrent of the Yangtze River in his mind's eye. Seeing before him this rare man who appreciated his otherwise hard-to-understand music, Boya was beside himself with joy. Instantly, the two became best friends. Before parting, they agreed to see each other again in the near future.

A few years later, Boya went to pay Zhong Ziqi a visit. Arriving at his home, Boya was told the sad news that that Zhong Ziqi had already passed away. Filled with deep sorrow, Boya lamented that no one in this world would ever be able to appreciate his music the way Zhong Ziqi had done. Rushing to his friend's grave, Boya dropped to his knees and started playing his *qin*. Then, rising slowly, he suddenly smashed the musical instrument onto the ground. From that day, no one ever heard or saw Boya playing a *qin* again.

This proverb is synonymous with a confidant or bosom friend who truly understands one's feelings. It also means a piece of good music, which is a definition at the proverb's face value.

# 高山流水

这条成语出自《列子·汤问》，《列子》是一部道学典籍，相传由与书名同名的列子撰写。列子，又叫列御寇，是5世纪中国的道家哲学家。

俞伯牙是春秋时期（公元前770－476年）楚国的著名音乐家。他自幼显露出音乐的<u>才华</u>，后来拜著名古琴演奏家成连为师。伯牙熟练地掌握了师傅传授给他的演奏<u>技艺</u>，但是仍不满意，感觉无法用琴来<u>充分</u>表达出自己内心的感受。成连遂将其带至东海的一个岛上，说是去见他自己的师傅。成连让伯牙耐心地等待他的师傅，说与他师傅见面以后会回来接他。几天过去了，伯牙连成连师傅的影子都看不到，成连本人也不知<u>去向</u>。

现在，只有岛上林子里的鸟儿与伯牙为伴。鸟儿的歌声伴随着海浪拍岸时的轰鸣构成美妙的交响曲，一下子打动了伯牙的心弦。伯牙叹了口气，弹奏起他的古琴来，悠扬的乐声带给他的正是他多日来苦苦追寻的那种感觉。其实，这正是师傅成连的<u>妙计</u>。后来人们发现，伯牙弹琴的时候，就连马厩里正在吃草的马都会扬起脖子聆听。然而，伯牙还是闷闷不乐，因为他觉得能够听懂他音乐的人<u>寥寥无几</u>。

一天，伯牙乘船外出，途中遇雨，只好停泊在岸边山脚下暂避。看着雨滴洒落在<u>荡漾</u>的河面上，伯牙禁不住坐在船上操起琴来。他边弹边<u>沉浸</u>在乐曲制造的情感<u>氛围</u>中，弹着、弹着，琴弦断了一根。伯牙抬起头来，<u>偶然</u>看到一个樵夫坐在岸边听得<u>如痴如醉</u>，居然连雨都不顾了。伯牙深受感动，急忙邀请这个叫钟子期的樵夫来到船上，继续演奏音乐给他听。伯牙刚刚奏完一首在他心中描绘高山的曲子，钟子期就脱口而出，说曲子让他想到<u>连绵不断</u>的大山。伯牙接着又弹奏了一段描绘流水的曲子，钟子期说他听到了湍急的江水。遇到<u>知音</u>，伯牙<u>喜出望外</u>，他们相见恨晚，临别时相约不久再见。

几年后，伯牙决定去探望钟子期。不幸的是，到了他家，却得到他已经去世的<u>噩耗</u>。伯牙<u>悲痛欲绝</u>，<u>凄凉</u>地感叹道，世上从此再无像钟子期那样能够欣赏其琴声的人了。他三步并作两步赶到子期的坟前，抚琴弹了一曲，然后慢慢地站起来，<u>猛地</u>把琴摔碎在地上。自此，再也听不到也看不到伯牙弹琴了。

这条成语几乎与"知音"、"至交"同义，也就是真正能够理解一个人的内心的人。该成语的另外一个意思与字面的意思接近，即一曲十分美妙的音乐。

## Vocabulary

| Characters | Pinyin | Word Type | Translation |
| --- | --- | --- | --- |
| 典籍 | diǎnjí | N. | classic book, ancient record |
| 才华 | cáihuá | N. | talent |
| 技艺 | jìyì | N. | skill, technique |
| 去向 | qùxiàng | N. | the direction where one is gone, whereabouts |
| 妙计 | miàojì | N. | a brilliant idea |
| 寥寥无几 | liáo liáo wú jǐ | ADJ. | very few |
| 荡漾 | dàngyàng | V. | to ripple |
| 沉浸 | chénjìn | V. | to immerse |
| 氛围 | fēnwéi | N. | atmosphere |
| 偶然 | ǒurán | ADJ./ADV. | accident; by accident, accidentally |
| 如痴如醉 | rú chī rú zuì | EXPR. | to be enthralled |
| 连绵不断 | lián mián bù duàn | ADJ./ADV. | endless; incessantly |
| 知音 | zhīyīn | N. | an appreciating friend, bosom friend |
| 喜出望外 | xǐ chū wàng wài | V. | to be overjoyed, to be pleasantly surprised |
| 相见恨晚 | xiāng jiàn hèn wǎn | EXPR. | to regret not having met sooner |
| 噩耗 | èhào | N. | bad news |
| 悲痛欲绝 | bēi tòng yù jué | EXPR. | to be extremely grieved |
| 凄凉 | qīliáng | ADJ. | mournful |
| 猛 | měng | ADV. | suddenly and vehemently |

## Examples

<u>高山流水</u>，知音难觅，人生得一知己足以。

Just as it is hard to find **a real connoisseur of a great music**, so too it is difficult to have a bosom friend. It's good enough to have one such friend in a lifetime.

这位钢琴家演奏的乐曲，有如<u>高山流水</u>，听得人如痴如醉。

This pianist played **such a beautiful melody** that it mesmerized the entire audience.

# Fiery Eyes with Golden Pupils

| 火 | 眼 | 金 | 睛 |
|---|---|---|---|
| huǒ | yǎn | jīn | jīng |
| fire | eye | gold | eye |

**Literal translation:** Fire eye gold eye.

**Meaning:** Having penetrating eyesight or perception.

**English equivalent:** To be eagle-eyed.

This proverb comes from the story of the Chinese mythological figure Sun Wukong, also known as the Monkey King, having his eyes turned into a fiery golden color. The first reference to this proverb occurs in *The Journey to the West Variety Show*, written by Yang Jingxian who lived in the late Yuan and early Ming dynasties. But it was Wu Cheng'en (1501–1582) who truly popularized the story in his classic Ming dynasty novel *Journey to the West*, which featured the Monkey King as a prominent character.

火
眼
金
睛

## Fiery Eyes with Golden Pupils

Monkey King had all sorts of tricks up his sleeve. He learned from a Daoist master how to transform himself into seventy-two different shapes and how to travel 108,000 *li* (or 33,550 miles) with a single somersault. His gold-ringed iron rod, which he took from the Dragon King of the East Sea, was a formidable weapon, weighing a thousand pounds and changing size at its owner's will.

The incident that got Monkey King his fiery eyes began at the Celestial Palace of the Jade Emperor of Heaven. Monkey King rebelled against the palace, but when the rebellion failed, the Jade Emperor of Heaven sentenced him to death by brutal corporal punishment. Monkey King's magic powers, however, enabled him to survive all methods of execution. At his wit's end, the emperor finally approved a proposal by a master alchemist to melt Monkey King in his elixir-making furnace.

Still, Monkey King defied any means of destruction. Instead of killing him, the furnace's smoke and fire only caused his pupils to turn fiery gold and his eyes became exceptionally perceptive—so much so that he could see through monsters no matter how they disguised themselves.

Fast forward five centuries (for a Monkey King lives a long time), and Monkey King, along with a motley crew of other characters, was now accompanying a monk named Tang Seng on a journey west to retrieve Buddhist texts. With his magical eyesight, Monkey King saw through many a phantom and demon disguised as innocent people. The most famous example of this occurred during a fight he had with a character named Baigujing (White Bone Spirit). Baigujing was bent on eating Tang Seng's flesh because whoever did this would, it was believed, gain eternal life. When Baigujing tried to capture Tang Seng by shape-shifting into a young woman, her mother, and her father successively, Monkey King sprang to his master's aid, killing this disguised spirit with his magic gold-ringed rod.

Eventually, Tang Seng, Monkey King, and the others resumed their journey west, and although they encountered many more perilous situations, with Monkey King by their side, these were but harmless adventures for Tang Seng and his disciples.

This proverb refers to a person's insight into what is truth and what is false.

# 火眼金睛

这则成语与美猴王孙悟空的眼睛变化有关。元朝杂剧作家杨景贤在其《西游记杂剧》中第一次提到了"火眼金睛"。杨景贤的生卒年月不详,大约生活在元顺帝(1320-1370)至明永乐帝(1360-1424年)的年代。然而,让这个成语家喻户晓的却是明朝的吴承恩(1501-1582),即著名文学典籍《西游记》的作者。

孙悟空,也叫美猴王,神通广大。他从一个道士那里学到七十二变的法术,也学会了筋斗云,一翻就是十万八千里。他从东海龙王那里取得的金箍棒,重达千钧,伸缩自如,是他克敌制胜的法宝。

美猴王反了天庭、大闹天宫失败以后,玉皇大帝用尽残酷的刑罚欲将他处死,但都因为美猴王施展出法力而不能得逞。玉皇无计可施,只好听从太上老君的建议,把他扔进老君的炼丹炉里融化掉。然而,什么都不能夺走美猴王的生命。炼丹炉非但没能把他杀死,其烟熏火燎,反而把美猴王的眼睛变成了火眼金睛,能够神奇地看穿一切妖魔鬼怪的千变万化。

一晃,五百年过去了,美猴王成了东土大唐高僧玄奘的徒弟,与其他几个徒弟一道,护送他去西天取经。一路上,美猴王用火眼金睛剥掉无数妖怪的伪装。其中最有名的一个故事,就是"三打白骨精"。白骨精听说吃了唐僧肉会长生不老,便一心想捉住唐僧,为此先后变幻成一个年轻女子、一个自称她母亲的老婆婆、还有一个自称她父亲的老伯。美猴王把白骨精的幻象一一看穿,并用金箍棒把他们全部击杀。

打打杀杀过后,师徒这才得以继续上路。一路上他们经历了无数艰难险阻,但是有美猴王护佑在唐僧的身旁,每一次历险都只不过是对唐僧意志的考验。

这条成语指的是一个人辨别真伪的洞察力。

## Vocabulary

| Characters | Pinyin | Word Type | Translation |
|---|---|---|---|
| 眼睛 | yǎnjīng | N. | eyes |
| 家喻户晓 | jiā yù hù xiǎo | EXPR. | well-known, understood by all |
| 即 | jí | ADV./ADJ. | namely, that is |
| 神通广大 | shéntōng guǎngdà | EXPR./ADJ. | to have magical powers or special talents |
| 筋斗云 | jīndǒuyún | N. | Monkey King's magical cloud |
| 金箍棒 | jīngūbàng | N. | golden-ringed rod (Monkey King's weapon) |
| 伸缩自如 | shēnsuō zì rú | EXPR. | to stretch smoothly, become short and long |
| 克敌制胜 | kè dí zhì shèng | V./EXPR. | to overcome your enemy and secure a victory |
| 残酷 | cánkù | ADJ./N. | cruel; cruelty |
| 施展 | shīzhǎn | V. | to exhaust, to fully use |
| 得逞 | déchéng | V. | to succeed |
| 无计可施 | wújìkěshī | EXPR. | to be at ones wit's end |
| 炼丹炉 | liàndānlú | N. | furnace used to make immortality pills |
| 融 | róng | V. | to melt |
| 然而 | ránér | ADV. | however |
| 夺走 | duózǒu | V. | to take away |
| 烟熏火燎 | yān xūn huǒ liǎo | EXPR. | surrounded by smoke and fire |
| 妖魔鬼怪 | yāo mó guǐ guài | EXPR./N. | demons and ghosts |
| 一晃 | yīhuǎng | CONJ. | in a flash |
| 护送 | hùsòng | V. | to escort |
| 西天取经 | xītiān qǔ jīng | EXPR. | to travel to the West (lit. the western paradise, India) to collect (Buddhist) classics; fig. to learn from somebody else's experience |
| 剥掉 | bōdiào | V. | to strip off |
| 妖怪 | yāoguài | N. | devil, ghost |
| 伪装 | wèizhuāng | N./V. | disguise; to pretend to be |
| 幻象 | huànxiàng | N. | illusion |

| Characters | Pinyin | Word Type | Translation |
|---|---|---|---|
| 得以 | déyǐ | V. | to enable; so that…can… |
| 艰难险阻 | jiānnán xiǎnzǔ | EXPR. | to face all kinds of dangers and difficulties |
| 意志 | yìzhì | N. | willpower |
| 辨别 | biànbié | V. | to differentiate, distinguish |
| 真伪 | zhēnwěi | N. | true or false, authenticity |
| 洞察力 | dòngchálì | N. | insight |

## Examples

便衣警察老李称得上是<u>火眼金睛</u>，毒贩很难从他眼下逃脱。

Plainclothes police officer Li is regarded **as having penetrating insight**: drug traffickers find it hard to escape his close watch.

她练就一双<u>火眼金睛</u>，假钞一眼就能看出来。

Her training has given her **a set of sharp eyes**. Now she can tell a counterfeit note at a glance.

# Who Can Untie the Bell from the Tiger's Neck?

| 解 | 铃 | 还 | 须 | 系 | 铃 | 人 |
|---|---|---|---|---|---|---|
| jiě | líng | hái | xū | xì | líng | rén |
| to untie | bell | also, still | must, have to | to tie | bell | person |

**Literal translation:** The person who unties the bell must also be the one who tied it.

**Meaning:** Whoever creates a difficult situation must resolve it himself.

The proverb derives from a story in the *Record of Alluding to the Moon* by Qu Ruji (1548–1610), an official of the Ming dynasty (1368–1644).

解铃还须系铃人

## Who Can Untie the Bell from the Tiger's Neck?

There once was a famous Buddhist monk named Fadeng in a temple on Mt. Qingliang in the vicinity of today's Nanjing. When he was young, Fadeng didn't seem to study as hard as his fellow monks, and for that reason they all looked down upon him. The abbot Fayan, however, liked him very much because he realized that Fadeng possessed an extraordinary capacity for comprehension. He was convinced that with this potential, the young man would become a great monk in due course.

One day, Abbot Fayan was giving a sermon to the monks. As usual, the young Fadeng was absent. During the discourse, Fayan raised a strange question. "A tiger has a bell tied to its neck. Who do you think would be able to untie it?" This query caught the monks by surprise. As they looked at one another in bewilderment, Fadeng stepped in. Abbot Fayan then asked him the same question. Without hesitation, the young monk replied, "It must be the one who tied the bell to the neck of the tiger." Turning to the other monks, the abbot commented, "I told you not to despise him. Trust me. He will be more successful than all of you in the days to come." Sure enough, Fadeng later became not only an accomplished abbot but also a great writer.

This proverb tells us that if we create a problem, we should be the one to solve it because we probably know more about it than anyone else and are most able to come up with a good solution.

# 解铃还须系铃人

这个成语源自明朝(公元1368－1644)一个叫瞿汝稷（公元1548-1610）的官员撰写的《指月录》。

　　古时候，今日南京城不远处，有座叫清凉的<u>丘陵</u>，丘陵上坐落着一<u>幢</u>庙，庙里有个<u>闻名天下</u>的法灯和尚。法灯年轻的时候，学习似乎没有他的小伙伴们那样努力，因此常常受到他们的<u>奚落</u>。法眼<u>住持</u>却很喜欢法灯，觉得他有<u>悟性</u>，将来一定会<u>前途无量</u>。法眼<u>笃信</u>，假以时日，法灯一定会出息成一个了不起的和尚。

　　一天，法眼住持在给和尚们讲经。法灯和往常一样没有到场。法眼住持讲着讲着问了大家一个问题，"有只老虎，脖子上系了一个铃铛。你们想一想，谁才能把铃铛解下来？"在座的和尚听了<u>一愣</u>，你看看我，我看看你，不知如何回答是好。正在此时，法灯走了进来。法眼住持于是把同样的问题又问了法灯一遍。这个小和尚<u>毫不迟疑</u>地回答道，"能把铃铛解下来的，一定是把它系到老虎脖子上的那个人。"法眼住持转过头来看着那些和尚说，"我早就跟你们讲过，不要看不起他。不信<u>等着瞧</u>，他将来会比你们任何一个人都有出息。"正如法眼住持<u>所料</u>，法灯后来不仅成为一名高僧，而且还是一个伟大的作家。

　　这则成语告诉我们，自己造成的问题，应由自己去解决，因为只有自己对问题的实质最了解，解决起来也最有办法。

## Vocabulary

| Characters | Pinyin | Word Type | Translation |
| --- | --- | --- | --- |
| 丘陵 | qiūlíng | N. | hills |
| 幢 | zhuàng | M. | measure word for large buildings |
| 闻名天下 | wén míng tiān xià | EXPR. | lit. a name heard all under heaven; fig. to be very famous |
| 奚落 | xīluò | V. | to scoff at; taunt; tease |
| 住持 | zhùchí | N. | (Buddhist or Daoist) abbot |
| 悟性 | wùxìng | N. | power of understanding |
| 前途无量 | qián tú wú liàng | EXPR. | to have a great future |
| 笃信 | dǔxìn | V. | to firmly believe, to be convinced of something |
| 一愣 | yīlèng | V. | to be taken aback |
| 毫不迟疑 | háo bù chí yí | ADV./EXPR. | without any doubt |
| 等着瞧 | děngzheqiáo | V. | to wait and see |
| 所料 | suǒliào | ADJ. | expected |

# Who Can Untie the Bell from the Tiger's Neck? * 解铃还须系铃人

## Examples

甲：能帮我个忙吗?

乙：什么事儿?

甲：能替我给她道个歉吗?

乙：<u>解铃还需系铃人</u>嘛。我看你还是亲自去道歉吧，她会原谅你的。

A: Could you do me a favor?

B: What's up?

A: I'd like you to apologize to her on my behalf.

B: **Whoever has a problem is the one who can best resolve it**. I think you'd better go and apologize to her yourself. She will forgive you.

中国认为，钓鱼岛争端是由日本购岛引起的，所以，"<u>解铃还需系铃人</u>"，改善两国关系的责任在日本一方。

China maintains that the dispute over the Diaoyu (Senkaku) Islands has been caused by Japan's purchasing it and that it is therefore Japan's responsibility to resolve it. As the saying goes, the **one who tied the bell to the tiger has to be the one to untie it**.

# Thick Willows and Colorful Bloom

| 柳 | 暗 | 花 | 明 |
|---|---|---|---|
| *liǔ* | *àn* | *huā* | *míng* |
| willow | dark | flower | bright |

**Literal translation:** Willows thick and flowers bright.

**Meaning:** An enchanting sight in spring time; a metaphor for a difficult situation taking a turn for the better.

**English equivalent:** Light at the end of the tunnel.

This proverb comes from two sources. It first appeared in the poem "Seeing Li Yuzhi Off to Fengxiang at Mohechi" by Wu Yuanheng (758–815), a chancellor during the reign of the Emperor Xianzong of the Tang dynasty. It was, however, Lu You (1125–1210), a prolific poet of the Song dynasty, who etched the proverb into the Chinese mind with his poem "A Visit to Mountain West Village." In Chinese literary history, Lu You has left the most poems, a total of 9,300.

## Thick Willows and Colorful Bloom

During the Southern (or Later) Song dynasty (1127–1279), the Jurchen Jin, a nomadic people from what is currently northeastern China, pushed the Song court out of northern Chinese territory and took it for themselves. The Song court relocated to South China, where they eventually chose Hangzhou to be its capital. There, Lu You adamantly advocated for the expulsion of the Jurchen Jin from the occupied north. For that, he lost favor in the Southern Song court dominated by capitulationists. Eventually he grew tired of political life and retreated to the country, where he could indulge himself in farming, drinking, and writing poetry.

He settled down by the Mirror Lake of Sanshan Village in present-day Zhejiang Province. One early spring day, he traveled to a neighboring village named Shanxi (West Side of the Mountain). Later, he recorded the experience in his poem:

> Don't laugh at farmers' murky wine brewed for the New Year;
> There's plenty of chicken and pork for guests after a harvest.
> Hill after hill and stream after stream, a path seems hard to find;
> Suddenly I see the village through thick willows and colorful blooms.
> Pipes and drums following me signal the coming Chunshe Festival;
> In robes and caps plain, people are sticking to their ancient folkway.
> From now on, if allowed and if I've time, every a moonlit night,
> Back on my walking stick, I'll knock at doors without your invite.

The proverb "thick willows and colorful blooms" is taken from the line "Suddenly I see the village through thick willows and colorful blooms," describing the beauty of the village ahead on a spring day. Today, however, it has become a metaphor for suddenly breaking through to success after a lot of difficulties, or seeing the light at the end of a tunnel.

# 柳暗花明

这条成语有两个出处，一是《摩河池送李侍御之凤翔》一诗，为唐宪宗时宰相武元衡（785－815）所作；另一个是宋代大诗人陆游（1125－1210）所做的名诗《游山西村》。陆游是中国文学史上现存诗歌最多的诗人，共有9,300首之多。正是陆游的这首诗使这条成语铭刻在每个中国人的心中。

1127年女真人建立的金国攻陷宋朝首都开封，大宋朝廷迁至中国南方，设首都于建康（即今日之南京），后又转迁临安（今日之杭州）。新建立的宋朝史称南宋（1127－1279）。在南宋朝廷做官的陆游一向坚持其收复失地，遂招致朝廷不悦。陆游最终厌倦政治斗争，告辞隐退，过起了田园生活，每天以饮酒赋诗为乐。

陆游辞去江西判官的官职后，落户在浙江山阴县镜湖附近的三山村。腊月的一天，他走访了附近的山西村。后来，他写了首诗，把这次走访的经历和感受记录了下来。诗云：

> 莫笑农家腊酒浑，
> 丰年留客足鸡豚。
> 山重水复疑无路，
> 柳暗花明又一村。
> 箫鼓追随春社近，
> 衣冠简朴古风存。
> 从今若许闲乘月，
> 柱杖无时夜叩门。

这条成语摘自诗中"柳暗花明又一村"一句，本意是描述前面村庄的美好风景，后借喻经历重重困难后，形势突然开始好转。

## Vocabulary

| Characters | Pinyin | Word Type | Translation |
|---|---|---|---|
| 柳暗花明 | liǔ àn huā míng | EXPR. | seeing light at the end of the tunnel |
| 铭刻 | míngkè | V. | to engrave, to etch |
| 收复失地 | shōu fù shī dì | EXPR. | to regain lost territory |
| 招致 | zhāozhì | V. | to lead to |
| 厌倦 | yànjuàn | V. | to be fed up with |
| 告辞 | gàocí | V. | to quit, say goodbye |
| 隐退 | yǐntuì | V. | to retire (from political life) |
| 田园 | tiányuán | N. | countryside |
| 以…为乐 | yǐ…wéilè | EXPR. | to take pleasure in |
| 赋诗 | fùshī | V. | to write poetry |
| 辞去 | cíqù | V. | to quit, to resign |
| 判官 | pánguàn | N. | magistrate |
| 腊月 | làyuè | N. | the twelfth month of the lunar calendar |
| 经历 | jīnglì | N./V. | experience; to experience |
| 感受 | gǎnshòu | N./V. | feeling; to experience |
| 莫 | mò | V. | do not; archaic word for 不, 没 |
| 浑 | hún | ADJ. | murky |
| 春社 | chūnshè | PN. | an ancient Chinese festival featuring the worship of the God of Soil and Ground |
| 衣冠 | yīguān | N. | attire, hat and clothes |
| 古风 | gǔfēng | N. | ancient folkway |

## Examples

失业半年，眼看无法生活下去，想不到<u>柳暗花明</u>，竟获得这件美差。

After being out of job for half a year, I was close to not being able to make ends meet. But as a saying goes, "**Things can turn on a dime**." Who could have imagined that I would land such a plum job?

不要因为一时的挫折而怀忧丧志，只要持续努力，总会有<u>柳暗花明</u>的时刻。

Don't be disheartened by temporary failures. So long as you do your best, **there's always a chance of success**.

# The Wind Ignores the Trees' Wishes

| 树 | 欲 | 静 | 而 | 风 | 不 | 止 |
|---|---|---|---|---|---|---|
| shù | yù | jìng | ér | fēng | bù | zhǐ |
| tree | to desire | quiet | but | wind | no, not | to stop |

**Literal translation:** The trees desire calm but the wind won't stop.

**Meaning:** Time waits for no man; things—good or bad—will happen, like it or not.

This proverb comes from two sources. One is Family Sayings of Confucius attributed to Kong Anguo (c. 156–74 BCE), a descendant of Confucius and a Confucian scholar and government official of the Western Han dynasty. A later Confucian scholar and government official of the Eastern Han dynasty, Wang Su (195–256 CE), edited it into twenty volumes, only ten of which have survived. Some argue, however, that the work was a fake done at a later time. Another source of the proverb is the Outer Commentary to the Book of Songs by Han Ying (c. 200–130 BCE) of the Han dynasty. The book is a medley of 360 anecdotes, moral stories, and practical advice.

# The Wind Ignores the Trees' Wishes

The story goes that Confucius was traveling with some of his disciples when he heard someone weeping with deep sorrow. "Hurry! Speed up the carriage! There must be a sage ahead of us," Confucius said. When he approached the man, Confucius recognized him as Gao Yu, well known at the time for being filially obedient and dutiful to his parents. He was crying by the roadside, wearing rough clothes and holding a sickle in his hands. Confucius got out of his carriage and asked, "Why are you crying with such sorrow? Are you mourning someone in your family?"

Gao Yu replied, "I committed three sins. First, I wasted my youth roaming from one state to another to pursue my studies when I should have used it to take care of my parents. Second, I was too proud to offer my service to His Majesty and so I have failed to contribute to the state. Lastly, I have alienated a lot of my bosom friends. The tree may yearn for calm, but the wind won't subside; the son may want to show love for his parents, but they have already passed away. Time can't be retrieved when it has elapsed; loved ones can't be seen again when they are gone. Please allow me to leave this world to join my dear departed." With that, he breathed his last breath and dropped dead.

"All of you should learn a lesson from what he has said. You need to understand the truth in it," Confucius turned to his disciples and said, whereupon about a third of them quit and went back home to take care of their parents.

Used alone, this proverb expresses the fact that things happen and time passes with no regard for human desire. Another meaning is that one party may want something to stop, but the other party won't allow it. If the proverb is combined with the saying "the children want to take care of the parents, but the parents have already gone," then it becomes a warning: we must act filial toward our parents before they pass away, because then it will be too late.

# 树欲静而风不止

该成语有两个出处。一说是《孔子家语》这部记述孔子思想和生平的著作。有人说原作者为孔子的后代、西汉学者官员孔安国（约公元前156 - 74 BC年），后来东汉人王肃（195 - 256年）将其整理成二十七卷，现存十卷；还有人说《孔子家语》是后人的伪作。另一个出处是《韩诗外传》，是一部由360条趣闻轶事、道德说教、伦理规范以及实际忠告等不同内容混编而成的书，作者为汉朝韩婴（约前200年 - 前130年）。

孔子出行，听到有人哭得十分悲伤。孔子说："快赶车，快赶车，前面有贤人。"走近一看是皋鱼，身披粗布抱着镰刀，在道旁哭泣。孔子下车对皋鱼说："你家里莫非有丧事？为什么哭得如此悲伤？"

皋鱼回答说："我有三个过失：年少时为了求学，周游诸侯国，以致耽误了赡养双亲的时间，这是过失之一。我自视清高，不愿为君主效力，对君上和国家没有贡献，这是过失之二。和朋友交情深厚却很早就断绝了来往，这是过失之三。'树欲静而风不止，子欲养而亲不待'，也就是说，树想静下来可风却不停，子女想好好赡养父母可父母却不在了！过去而不能追回的是岁月，逝去而再也见不到的是亲人。请允许我从此离别人世，去陪伴逝去的亲人吧。"说着就溘然辞世了。

孔子对弟子们说："你们要引以为戒，这件事足以使你们明白其中的道理！"于是，辞行回家赡养双亲的门徒十之有三。

这条成语单用的时候，是取其引申的意义，即事物的发展或时间的流逝是不以人的意志为转移的客观规律；其进一步引申为，一方想停止做某事，而另一方却不让其停止。如果和"子欲养而亲不待"一起联用的话，则是从反面来告诫人们，要趁着父母健在的时候行孝，等到父母去世了就来不及了。

## Vocabulary

| Characters | Pinyin | Word Type | Translation |
| --- | --- | --- | --- |
| 伪作 | wěizuò | N. | counterfeit |
| 趣闻轶事 | qù wén yì shì | N. | anecdote |
| 道德说教 | dàodé shuōjiào | EXPR./V. | to moralize; moralization |
| 伦理规范 | lún lǐ guī fàn | EXPR./N. | ethical norms |
| 混编 | hùnbiān | V. | to mix different material in a compilation |
| 贤人 | xiánrén | N. | a person of virtue |
| 耽误 | dānwu | V. | to delay, to hold up |
| 赡养 | shànyǎng | V. | to support, to provide for (one's children and parents) |
| 效力 | xiàolì | V. | to serve, to render service to |
| 自视清高 | zì shì qīng gāo | V. | to have a good opinion of oneself |
| 贡献 | gòngxiàn | N./V | contribution; to contribute |
| 欲 | yù | MOD. V. | will, would like to, want to |
| 溘然 | kèrán | ADV. | suddenly |
| 引以为戒 | yǐn yǐ wéi jiè | EXPR./V. | to learn a lesson |
| 辞世 | cíxíng | V. | to pass away |
| 引申 | yǐnshēn | V. | to extend in meaning |
| 趁着 | chènzhe | CONJ. | while (a favorable condition is still available) |
| 健在 | jiànzài | V. | (of a person, particularly of advanced age) to be still living and in good health |
| 行孝 | xíngxiào | V. | to fulfill filial duty |
| 来不及 | láibují | EXPR. | it's too late, there's not enough time |

## Examples

我想自己忍一忍，道个歉就算了，可是<u>树欲静而风不止</u>啊，她却纠缠不休。

I thought that everything would be fine after I apologized and put up with the humiliation; but she kept badgering me **like gusts of wind that refuse to subside**.

"<u>树欲静而风不止</u>，子欲养而亲不待"，故行孝当及时，一旦错过机会，将追悔莫及。

**Like the gusting wind that cares not if a tree wants calm**, time marches on and our parents can pass away before we start thinking of returning their love. We must act now before it's too late, or we'll be left with nothing but regret.

# A Promise Is Worth a Thousand Pieces of Gold

| 一 | 诺 | 千 | 金 |
|---|---|---|---|
| *yī* | *nuò* | *qiān* | *jīn* |
| one | to promise | thousand | gold |

**Literal translation:** one promise, a thousand teals of gold.

**Meaning:** We must keep our promises; we have to be as good as our word.

This proverb comes from the famous *Records of the Grand Historian*, a monumental history of ancient China covering a time from the era of the Yellow Emperor to the fourth year of Emperor Wu's reign in the Western Han dynasty (206–8 BCE), a span of three thousand years. The book is attributed to father and son Sima Tan and Sima Qian, who successively served as astronomers and historiographers in the Han court.

## A Promise Is Worth a Thousand Pieces of Gold

This story takes place at the end of the Qin dynasty (221–206 BCE). In the State of Chu, there was a man named Ji Bu. Honest and generous, he never broke his promise no matter what difficulty would stand in the way. Therefore, everyone respected him. A war broke out for the crown of the Qin dynasty between the leaders of the two rebel armies led by Liu Bang and Xiang Yu. As a general of Xiang Yu, Ji Bu defeated Liu Bang many a time. Eventually, Liu Bang defeated Xiang Yu and became the founding emperor of the Han dynasty. He wanted to capture Ji Bu to avenge his previous defeats. Now a wanted fugitive, Ji Bu exiled himself.

Out of great respect for Ji Bu, a lot of people secretly helped him. One of them was Zhu Jia. He gave Ji Bu a temporary farmhand job by way of expediency and wasted no time in going to talk with Xiahou Ying, a minister of the Han court and a close friend of Liu Bang. He finally persuaded Xiahou Ying to realize that Ji Bu could be a great asset to the Han court. Xiahou Ying then convinced Liu Bang to revoke his decree to arrest Ji Bu. The emperor first made Ji Bu a vice minister and later appointed him to the governorship of Hedong Prefecture.

Cao Qiu was a fellow villager of Ji Bu, but the latter had been contemptuous of him for his snobbishness. Now that Ji Bu became a high-ranking official, Cao came to curry his favor by telling him, "I keep hearing a popular saying circulating in our hometown: 'A promise from Ji Bu is worth more than a thousand pieces of gold.'" Ji Bu was very pleased to hear the compliment and reconciled with Cao. It turned out that Cao worked hard to spread Ji Bu's reputation for keeping promises far and wide and won him more admiration.

This proverb praises the value of trustworthiness gained from keeping one's promises.

# 一诺千金

这条成语出自著名的《史记》。这部纪传体历史巨著,从黄帝时代写到汉武帝统治的第四个年头,跨度达3000年之久。这本书由司马谈(约公元前165－110年)和司马迁(公元前145－90年)父子编成,他们相继担任汉廷太史令。

故事发生在秦朝(公元前221-207)结束之前。楚国有个人叫季布,为人<u>耿直</u>,助人为乐。不管有多大困难,他都会说到做到,因此大家都非常敬重他。在楚汉之争的时候,季布为项羽效力,多次击败过刘邦。后来,项羽被刘邦打败,季布开始了<u>流亡</u>生活。已是汉朝开国皇帝的刘邦,总想抓到他,以雪屡败其手之恨。因此,季布一下子成了被<u>通缉</u>的逃犯。

出于对季布的敬重,很多人都在私底下向他伸出援手。其中就有一个叫朱家的人,出于<u>权宜之计</u>,暂时收留他在农田帮工,与此同时,便去找刘邦的好友夏侯婴<u>说情</u>。朱家告诉夏侯婴,季布会成为汉廷的<u>栋梁</u>之才。夏侯婴于是就去说服了刘邦,把对季布的通缉令<u>撤消</u>。<u>不仅如此</u>,刘邦还任命季布为<u>郎中</u>,后来又将其升为河东<u>太守</u>。

季布有个<u>同乡</u>叫曹丘,喜欢结交有权势的人。为此,季布向来<u>瞧不起</u>他。听说季布做了大官,曹丘又来<u>奉承</u>起他来,说,"我在老家听到人们到处在讲:'得黄金百两,不如得季布一诺'。"季布听后大喜,遂与曹丘<u>言归于好</u>。曹丘从此也到处宣扬季布一诺千金的<u>品格</u>,让他的名声越来越大。

这条成语<u>赞扬</u>了<u>遵守</u>诺言、<u>取信于人</u>的品格。

## Vocabulary

| Characters | Pinyin | Word Type | Translation |
| --- | --- | --- | --- |
| 耿直 | gěngzhí | ADJ. | honest, frank |
| 流亡 | liúwáng | V./ADJ. | to exile; exiled |
| 通缉 | tōngjī | V. | to order the arrest (of a criminal), to list as wanted |
| 权宜之计 | quán yí zhī jì | EXPR. | a temporary solution, a makeshift plan |
| 说情 | shuōqíng | V. | to plead for mercy for someone |
| 栋梁之才 | dòngliáng zhī cái | N. | a pillar of society |
| 撤销 | chèxiāo | V. | to revoke |
| 不仅如此…还（而且）… | bù jǐn rú cǐ…hái (érqiě)… | CONJ. | not only…but also… |
| 郎中 | lángzhōng | N. | ancient official title |
| 太守 | tàishǒu | N. | governor of a province |
| 奉承 | fèngchéng | V. | to flatter, to fawn upon |
| 言归于好 | yán guī yú hǎo | EXPR./V. | to bury the hatchet |
| 品格 | pǐngé | N. | character |
| 赞扬 | zànyáng | V. | to praise |
| 遵守 | zūnshǒu | V. | to obey |
| 取信于人 | qǔ xìn yú rén | V. | to win the trust or confidence of others |

## Examples

甲：你真是说话算话，谢谢你的帮助！

乙：没问题，君子<u>一诺千金</u>。

甲：你真是个可交的朋友！

A: You did what you said. Thank you for your help!

B: Welcome! **A promise is a promise**.

A: You are a friend indeed.

尽管这个产品价值高涨，但他还是按照我们原来商定的价格卖给了我。他真是<u>一诺千金</u>啊！

Despite the rapid increase in the value of the product, he still sold it to me at our original agreed-upon price. He is really **a man of his word**!

# A Pillow and a Pot of Congee

| 一 | 枕 | 黄 | 梁 |
|---|---|---|---|
| yī | zhěn | huáng | liáng |
| one | pillow | yellow | millet |

**Literal translation:** One pillow and yellow millet.

**Meaning:** A daydream or a fond hope.

**English equivalent:** A pipe dream.

This proverb originated from "The World Inside a Pillow," a traditional Tang dynasty (618–907 CE) short story written by Shen Jiji.

## A Pillow and a Pot of Congee

A travelling young man named Lu Sheng put up for the night at a tavern in Handan, where he met a Daoist priest, Lü Weng. As they chatted, the young man sighed and complained about his unfortunate life. He told Lü that he had failed the imperial civil service examination repeatedly despite his talent and diligence and was therefore still living in poverty. Hearing this, Lü Weng took a pillow out of his luggage. On it were embroidered the Chinese characters for "good luck," "official salary," and "long life" in addition to pictures of official headwear, a gold bar, a beautiful young woman, and several children. Handing the pillow to the young man, Lü Weng said, "You will find your happiness when you sleep on it."

While they were chatting, the owner of the tavern had started cooking a pot of millet congee. Seeing that it was still early for supper, Lu Sheng decided to take a nap. As soon as his head hit the pillow, he fell into a deep sleep. In his dream, he married a beautiful young woman from a rich family and soon passed the civil service examination. Then he became a magistrate and was eventually promoted to the position of prime minister. More than ten years of service in the court also earned him the title of duke. He had five sons, each of whom became an official and had a large family. The numerous grandchildren brought Lu Sheng infinite joy, and he lived happily into his eighties. Looking back at his past, Lu Sheng chuckled with satisfaction, and with that, he woke up, only to find the congee still simmering on the stove. Lu Sheng said to the Daoist priest with a sigh, "Well, years of a happy life are even shorter than the time it takes to cook a pot of millet." "You're right," said the priest. "Life is but a dream no matter how much you enjoy it. So why bother?" Hearing this, Lu Sheng suddenly and deeply comprehended this truth about life. Instead of continuing to pursue officialdom by taking imperial civil examinations, he converted to Daoism and became a recluse.

This proverb is a metaphor for fond hopes or pipe dreams, while the story behind the proverb expresses the view that moments are fleeting and all wonderful things—honor, wealth, high positions—eventually evaporate like a dream, similar to the sentiment expressed in the saying "all good things must come to an end."

# 一枕黄粱

这则成语出自唐代（公元618－907年）传奇作家沈既济的《枕中记》。

一个叫卢生的人，回家途中，路过邯郸时来到一个<u>客栈</u>，准备在那里过夜。在客栈里，他遇到一位叫吕翁的道士。与道士闲聊的时候，卢生唉声叹气地诉说了自己的<u>坎坷</u>。原来，尽管他<u>才华横溢</u>、勤学苦读，还是一次又一次地<u>落榜</u>，导致生活依然拮据。听着听着，吕翁从行囊中掏出一个枕头来。枕头上绣着"福、禄、寿"三个字，还绣着一顶<u>乌纱帽</u>、一根金条、一个漂亮的年轻女子，以及几个孩子。吕翁一边把枕头递给卢生，一边<u>说道</u>，"枕着这个枕头睡一觉，你就会找到你的幸福。"

他们聊天的时候，客栈老板正在熬着一锅小米粥。看看时间尚早，卢生决定在晚饭前小憩片刻。他头一挨着枕头，就沉睡了过去。睡梦中，他<u>娶</u>了一个漂亮的富家女，很快又考中进士，做了官，从县衙一直做到<u>宰相</u>，朝中贵为<u>公卿</u>十几年。他有了五个儿子，长大成人后，全都做了官，成了家，生了许多孩子。卢生子孙<u>绕膝</u>，尽享天伦之乐，幸福地活到八十多岁。回首往事，卢生<u>忍俊不禁</u>，结果把自己给笑醒了。睁眼一看，炉子上的一锅黄粱米粥尚未煮熟。卢生对道士长叹道："唉，幸福一生，居然不到煮一锅小米粥的时辰。"道士说，"你说对了！不管你能享受多少荣华富贵，生活也不过是一场梦而已。所以，有什么可以让你忧愁的呢？"听了道士的话，卢生<u>大彻大悟</u>，于是就不再<u>追逐</u>功名，做了道士并隐居起来。

这则成语对奢望或白日梦做了形象的比喻。成语背后表达了这样的观点，即：时间如白驹过隙，转瞬即逝，所以美好的事物，诸如荣誉、财富、高官厚禄等等，最终都像梦一样化为浮云。总之，天下没有不散的酒席。

## Vocabulary

| Characters | Pinyin | Word Type | Translation |
|---|---|---|---|
| 客栈 | kèzhàn | N. | tavern, guest house |
| 坎坷 | kǎnkě | ADJ./V. | bumpy, rough; to be down on one's luck |
| 才华横溢 | cái huá héng yì | EXPR./V. | to be brilliant, to have a lot of talent |
| 落榜 | luòbǎng | V. | to fail (the imperial exams) |
| 乌纱帽 | wūshāmào | N. | lit. crow yarn hat, a black hat specifically worn by officials; fig. official post |
| 娶 | qǔ | V. | to marry, to take a wife (only used for men) |
| 宰相 | zǎixiàng | N. | prime minister (official position in ancient China) |
| 公卿 | gōngqīng | N. | high ranking official at the court |
| 绕膝 | ràoxī | V. | lit. to run around someone's knees; fig. to take care of one's elderly parents |
| 忍俊不禁 | rěn jùn bù jīn | EXPR. | cannot help smiling or laughing |
| 大彻大悟 | dà chè dà wù | EXPR. | to achieve enlightenment or nirvana (Buddhism), to have an insight |
| 追逐 | zhuīzhú | V. | to chase, to pursue |

## Examples

甲：我哥哥从来也不好好学习，却天天想着做一个宇航员。

乙：他在作<u>一枕黄粱</u>美梦。

A: My brother never studies hard, but he is always thinking of becoming an astronaut.
B: He is **simply daydreaming**.

他虽中了乐透奖，但因花钱大手大脚，不久就一无所有了，乐透终成<u>一枕黄粱</u>梦。

He soon squandered away all the money he won from the lottery, and winning the lottery eventually **felt like just a dream**.

# Alphabetical List

**An tu suo ji** 按图索骥 | Using a Picture to Find a Horse (p. 157)
**Bai ju guo xi** 白驹过隙 | Seeing a Horse Whizzing by Through a Crack in the Wall (p. 161)
**Ba xian guo hai, ge xian qi neng** 八仙过海，各显其能 | Eight Immortals Crossing the Sea, Flaunting Their Magic Power (p. 165)
**Bei gong she ying** 杯弓蛇影 | Mistaking a Bow's Reflection for a Snake (p. 3)
**Bu ru huxue, yan de huzi** 不入虎穴，焉得虎子 | No Tiger's Den, No Tiger's Cub (p. 173)
**Dong shi xiao pin** 东施效颦 | Dong Shi Mimics a Frown (p. 75)
**Dui niu tan qin** 对牛弹琴 | Playing the Zither to a Cow (p. 9)
**Gao shan liu shui** 高山流水 | High Mountains, Flowing Water (p. 179)
**Handan xue bu** 邯郸学步 | Learning to Walk in Handan (p. 79)
**Houzi qiu yue** 猴子救月 | Monkeys Rescuing the Moon (p. 85)
**Hu jia hu wei** 狐假虎威 | The Fox Assuming the Power of the Tiger (p. 13)
**Hua long dian jing** 画龙点睛 | Adding Eyes to a Painted Dragon (p. 21)
**Huo yan jin jing** 火眼金睛 | Fiery Eyes with Golden Pupils (p. 187)
**Jiao tu san ku** 狡兔三窟 | A Cunning Rabbit Has Three Burrows (p. 91)
**Jie ling hai xu xi ling ren** 解铃还须系铃人 | Who Can Untie the Bell from the Tiger's Neck? (p. 193)
**Jingwei tian hai** 精卫填海 | Jingwei Fills Up the Sea (p. 25)
**Kai tian pi di** 开天辟地 | Heaven Separates from Earth (p. 29)
**Ke zhou qiu jian** 刻舟求剑 | Marking the Boat to Find Your Sword (p. 99)
**Lan yu chong shu** 滥竽充数 | A Fake Player in the Band (p. 105)
**Lao ma shi tu** 老马识途 | An Old Horse Knows the Way (p. 35)
**Li yu tiao long men** 鲤鱼跳龙门 | Aspiring to Become a Dragon (p. 111)
**Liu an hua ming** 柳暗花明 | Thick Willows and Colorful Bloom (p. 199)
**Qi ren you tian** 杞人忧天 | The Man from Qi Who Worries About the Sky (p. 115)
**Qian lü zhi ji** 黔驴之技 | Tricks of a Donkey (p. 39)
**Sai Weng shi ma** 塞翁失马 | A Horse Lost Is a Stable Gained (p. 119)
**San ren cheng hu** 三人成虎 | Three People Can Create a Tiger (p. 123)
**Shou zhu dai tu** 守株待兔 | Waiting for Another Hare to Come Your Way (p. 127)
**Shu yu jing er feng bu zhi** 树欲静而风不止 | The Wind Ignores the Trees' Wishes (p. 205)
**Tanglang bu chan, huangque zai hou** 螳螂捕蝉黄雀在后 | Catching a Cicada, Blind to the Oriole (p. 133)

**Tong zhou gong ji** 同舟共济 | Crossing the River in the Same Boat (p. 139)
**Wo xin chang dan** 卧薪尝胆 | Sleeping on Sticks and Eating Bile (p. 143)
**Ya miao zhu zhang** 揠苗助长 | Pulling Up Rice Shoots to Help Them Grow (p. 47)
**Ye gong hao long** 叶公好龙 | The Dragon Lover Lord Ye (p. 51)
**Yi jian shuang jiao** 一箭双雕 | Killing Two Birds with One Arrow (p. 147)
**Yi nuo qian jin** 一诺千金 | A Promise is Worth a Thousand Pieces of Gold (p. 211)
**Yi zhen huang liang** 一枕黄粱 | A Pillow and a Pot of Congee (p. 217)
**Yu bang xiang zheng, yu weng de li** 鹬蚌相争，渔翁得利 | The Fisherman Benefits from the Snipe Grappling with the Clam (p. 151)
**Yu gong yi shan** 愚公移山 | The Fool Set on Moving a Mountain (p. 57)
**Zheng ren mai lü** 郑人买履 | A Man from Zheng Shops for Shoes (p. 65)
**Zi xiang mao dun** 自相矛盾 | Your Own Spear Against Your Own Shield (p. 69)

# Topical List

## Art and Beauty

Adding Eyes to a Painted Dragon | *Hua long dian jing* 画龙点睛 (p. 21)
    **Meaning**: Adding the final touch to make a piece of art come to life
High Mountains, Flowing Water | *Gao shan liu shui* 高山流水 (p. 179)
    **Meaning**: A piece of truly great music; a bosom friend
Thick Willows and Colorful Bloom | *Liu an hua ming* 柳暗花明 (p. 199)
    **Meaning**: An enchanting sight in spring time

## Culture and Education

A Promise is Worth a Thousand Pieces of Gold | *Yi nuo qian jin* 一诺千金 (p. 211)
    **Meaning**: We must keep our promises
Playing the Zither to a Cow | *Dui niu tan qin* 对牛弹琴 (p. 9)
    **Meaning**: Casting pearls before a swine

## Emotions & Fear

Mistaking a Bow's Reflection for a Snake | *Bei gong she ying* 杯弓蛇影 (p. 3)
    **Meaning**: Being afraid because of imagined problems
Monkeys Rescuing the Moon | *Houzi qiu yue* 猴子救月 (p. 85)
    **Meaning:** Worrying over nothing
The Dragon Lover Lord Ye | *Ye gong hao long* 叶公好龙 (p. 51)
    **Meaning**: Professing love for what one actually fears
The Man from Qi Who Worries about the Sky | *Qi ren you tian* 杞人忧天 (p. 115)
    **Meaning**: To overact to groundless worries

## Knowledge & Skill

A Cunning Rabbit Has Three Burrows | *Jiao tu san ku* 狡兔三窟 (p. 91)
    **Meaning**: Having several ways of protecting oneself
An Old Horse Knows the Way | *Lao ma shi tu* 老马识途 (p. 35)
    **Meaning**: Use your experience or that of others

Crossing the River in the Same Boat | *Tong zhou gong ji* 同舟共济 (p. 139)
   **Meaning:** Working closely together to overcome difficulties
Eight Immortals Crossing the Sea, Flaunting Their Magic Power | *Baxian guo hai, ge xian qi neng* 八仙过海，各显其能 (p. 165)
   **Meaning:** Each person has a unique way of solving a problem
Fiery Eyes with Golden Pupils | *Huo yan jin jing* 火眼金睛 (p. 187)
   **Meaning:** To be eagle-eyed
Who Can Untie the Bell from the Tiger's Neck? | *Jie ling hai xu ji ling ren* 解铃还须系铃人 (p. 193)
   **Meaning:** Whoever creates a difficulty must resolve it
Tricks of a Donkey | *Qian lü zhi ji* 黔驴之技 (p. 39)
   **Meaning:** Having exhausted one's tactics or skills
Your Own Spear against Your Own Shield | *Zixiang maodun* 自相矛盾 (p. 69)
   **Meaning:** Contradicting oneself

## Perseverance

Aspiring to Become a Dragon | *Li yu tiao long men* 鲤鱼跳龙门 (p. 111)
   **Meaning:** Striving for success despite difficulties
Jingwei Fills Up the Sea | *Jingwei tian hai* 精卫填海 (p. 25)
   **Meaning:** Set on achieving one's goal despite difficulties
The Fool Set on Moving a Mountain | *Yu gong yi shan* 愚公移山 (p. 57)
   **Meaning:** Persevering in the face of difficulties
Sleeping on Sticks and Eating Bile | *Wo xin chang dan* 卧薪尝胆 (p. 143)
   **Meaning:** Enduring hardships to cultivate perseverance

## Pretending

A Fake Player in the Band | *Lan yu chong shu* 滥竽充数 (p. 105)
   **Meaning:** To be a makeweight
Dong Shi Mimics a Frown | *Dong shi xiao pin* 东施效颦 (p. 75)
   **Meaning:** Being a copycat
Learning to Walk in Handan | *Handan xue bu* 邯郸学步 (p. 79)
   **Meaning:** Losing your own individuality by imitating others
The Fox Assuming the Power of the Tiger | *Hu jia hu wei* 狐假虎威 (p. 13)
   **Meaning:** Assuming someone else's authority
Three People Can Create a Tiger | *San ren cheng hu* 三人成虎 (p. 123)
   **Meaning:** A lie, repeated often enough, is accepted as the truth

## Risks, Winning, and Losing

A Horse Lost Is a Stable Gained | *Sai Weng shi ma* 塞翁失马 (p. 119)
   **Meaning:** A blessing in disguise

Killing Two Birds with One Arrow | *Yi jian shuang jiao* 一箭双雕 (p. 147)
  **Meaning:** Accomplishing two goals with one action
Catching a Cicada, Blind to the Oriole | *Tanglang bu chan, huangque zai hou* 螳螂捕蝉黄雀在后 (p. 133)
  **Meaning:** Having a blind spot because you are focused on one thing only
No Tiger's Den, No Tiger's Cub | *Buru huxue, yande huzi* 不入虎穴，焉得虎子 (p. 173)
  **Meaning:** Nothing ventured, nothing gained
The Fisherman Benefits from the Snipe Grappling with the Clam | *Yu bang xiang zheng, yu weng de li* 鹬蚌相争，渔翁得利 (p. 151)
  **Meaning:** A dispute between two parties may only benefit a third party

## Stubbornness

A Man from Zheng Shops for Shoes | *Zheng ren mai lü* 郑人买履 (p. 65)
  **Meaning:** To bind yourself by old and nonfunctional practices
A Pillow and a Pot of Congee | *Yi zhen huang liang* 一枕黄粱 (p. 217)
  **Meaning:** A daydream or a fond hope
Marking the Boat to Find Your Sword | *Ke zhou qiu jian* 刻舟求剑 (p. 99)
  **Meaning:** Doing something the same way despite different circumstances
Pulling Up Rice Shoots to Help Them Grow | *Ya miao zhu zhang* 揠苗助长 (p. 47)
  **Meaning:** Spoiling something by being impatient and forcing ahead
Using a Picture to Find a Horse | *An tu suo ji* 按图索骥 (p. 157)
  **Meaning:** Being extremely rigid
Waiting for Another Hare to Come Your Way | *Shou zhu dai tu* 守株待兔 (p. 127)
  **Meaning:** Waiting for a lucky break without putting any effort in

## Time

Heaven Separates from Earth | *Kai tian pi di* 开天辟地 (p. 29)
  **Meaning:** Since the dawn of time, ground-breaking
Seeing a Horse Whizzing by Through a Crack in the Wall | *Bai ju guo xi* 白驹过隙 (p. 161)
  **Meaning:** Life is short and time flies
The Wind Ignores the Trees' Wishes | *Shu yu jing er feng bu zhi* 树欲静而风不止 (p. 205)
  **Meaning:** Good and bad things will happen regardless

# Glossary

*Art of War* (*Sunzi* 孙子). A military treaties authored by Sunzi.

Ban Chao 班超. Statesman and diplomat of the Eastern Han dynasty.

Ban Gu 班固 (32–92 CE). Historian of the Eastern Han dynasty, author of the *Book of Han*.

*Book of Jin* (*Jin Shu* 晋书). One of the Twenty-Four Histories of China. Compiled by Fang Xuanling (579–648 CE).

*Book of the Later Han* (*Hou Han Shu* 后汉书). Historical work written by Fan Ye 范晔 (398–445 CE).

Chen Shou 陈寿 (233–297 CE). An official from the state of Wu, author of *Records of the Three Kingdoms*.

chengyu 成语. A proverb.

*Classic of Mountains and Seas* (*Shan Hai Jing* 山海经). Mythical geographical and cultural account of China prior to the Qin dynasty.

Confucius 孔子 (551–479 BCE). Influential Spring and Autumn period philosopher.

dao 道. Philosophical (Daoist) concept referring to the Way (of the universe).

diangu 典故. Classical allusions or literary quotations.

Eight Immortals (*baxian* 八仙). Daoist concept of a group of ordinary men and women who became immortal.

Fang Xuanling 房玄龄 (579–648 CE). Co-compiler of the *Book of Jin* (*Jin Shu* 晋书).

*Forest of Gems in the Garden of the Dharma* (*Fa fan zhulin* 法苑珠林). Hundred-volume encyclopedia covering mainly Buddhist and some other ancient texts. Written by Dao Shi 道世 in 668 CE.

geyan 格言. Maxim, motto, or aphorism.

Gongsun Long 公孙龙 (c. 325–250 BCE). Philosopher, logician, and founder of the School of Names.

guanyongyu 惯用语. Commonly used phrase or a colloquial usage.

*Hanfeizi* 韩非子. Philosophical classic compiled by the philosopher Han Feizi.

Han Feizi 韩非子 (c. 280–233 BCE), also known as Han Fei or Master Fei. Warring States period legalist philosopher, essayist, and political commentator.

Han Ying 韩婴 (c. 200–130 BCE). Author of *The Outer Commentary to the Book of Songs*, a compilation of Han dynasty anecdotes, moral stories, and practical advice.

*The Historical Records of the Three Sovereigns and Five Emperors* (*Sanwu li ji* 三五历记). Historical record written by historian Xu Zheng during the Three Kingdoms period.

*The History of the Northern Dynasties* (*Beishi* 北史). Historical record that covers the period from 386 to 618 CE.

*Huainanzi* 淮南子. Philosophical text, attributed to Liu An (179–122 BCE).

Jinling 金陵. Present-day Nanjing.

Kong Anguo 孔安国 (c. 156–74 BCE). Descendant of Confucius and a Confucian scholar and government official of the Western Han dynasty, author of *Family Sayings of Confucius*.

Laozi 老子. A Daoist philosopher, presumed author of the *Daodejing*.

Liezi 列子, also known as Lie Yukou 列御寇. A fifth-century BCE Daoist philosopher from the state of Zheng.

*Liezi* 列子. Daoist classic attributed to its namesake Liezi.

Liu Xiang 刘向 (77–6 BCE). Western Han dynasty government official, scholar, writer, and compiler of the *Strategies of the Warring States*.

Liu Zongyuan 柳宗元 (773–819 CE). Author and founder of the Classical Prose Movement.

Lü Buwei 吕不韦 (291–235 BCE). Prime minister of the state of Qin during the Warring States period, author of *Mr. Lü's Spring and Autumn Annals*.

Lu You 陆游 (1125–1210). Song dynasty poet.

*Master Mou's Treatise on the Removal of Doubts* (*Mouzi li gan lun* 牟子理惑论). Allegedly China's first writing on Buddhism. The Master Mou in the title likely refers to Mou Rong.

Mencius (371–289 BCE), also known as Mengzi 孟子 (or Master Meng). Warring States period Confucian philosopher. Author of the *Gongsun Chou* 公孙丑.

*Mr. Lü's Spring and Autumn Annals* (*Lüshi Chunqiu* 吕氏春秋). Summary of the philosophical schools of Legalism, Confucianism, Mohism, and Daoism. Written by Lü Buwei and his disciples.

Mou Rong 牟融. Eastern Han dynasty scholar-official.

Ouyang Xiu 欧阳修 (1007–1072). Song dynasty scholar-official, author of *The Book of the New Tang*.

Ouyang Xun 欧阳询 (557–641 CE). Early Tang dynasty Confucian scholar and calligrapher, Compiler of the encyclopedic work *Collection of Literature by Category*.

Pangu 盘古. Mythical bird-like creature, believed to be the creator of the world.

*qin* (or *guqin*) 古琴. A traditional Chinese stringed instrument of the zither family.

Qu Ruji 瞿汝稷 (1548–1610). Ming dynasty official, author of *Record of Alluding to the Moon*.

*Records of the Grand Historian* (*Shiji* 史记). Monumental history of ancient China covering a span of 3,000 years, from the Yellow Emperor to the Western Han dynasty. Attributed to Sima Tan and his son, Sima Qian.

*Records of the Three Kingdoms* (*Sanguo zhi* 三国志). An historical text covering the period 220–265 CE, written by the official Chen Shou 陈寿 (233–297 CE).

Shen Jiji 沈既济. Tang dynasty author of the short story *The World Inside a Pillow*.

*shuyu* 熟语. Generic word for Chinese set phrases and expressions.

Sima Qian 司马迁 (c. 145–86 BCE). Han dynasty court astronomer and historian. Co-author (with his father Sima Tan) of *Records of the Grand Historian*, and considered the father of Chinese historiography.

*Strategies of the Warring States* (*Zhuanguo ce* 战国策). Treatise on political strategists and historical and social characteristics of the period. Generally attributed to Liu Xiang, but sometimes claimed to have been written by Kuai Tong, a strategist from the Qin dynasty.

Sun Wukong 孙悟空, also known as the Monkey King. Character from Wu Cheng'en's novel *Journey to the West*.

Sunzi 孙子 (544–496 BCE), also known as Sun Wu 孙武 or Master Sun. A famous war strategist of the Spring and Autumn period, author of the *Art of War*.

Wu Cheng'en 吴承恩 (c. 1501–1582). Ming dynasty writer, author of *Journey to the West*.

Wu Yuantai 吴元泰. Ming dynasty Daoist writer, author of *Journey to the East*.

Xi Shi 西施. Renowned beauty from the state of Yue during the Spring and Autumn period.

*xiehouyu* 歇后语. Two-part allegorical saying.

Xiongnu 匈奴. Confederation of nomadic people living on the Asian steppe, who raided China from time to time throughout history.

Xu Zheng 徐整 (220–280 CE). Historian from the Three Kingdoms period (220–265 CE), author of *The Historical Records of the Three Sovereigns and Five Emperors* 三五历记.

*yanyu* 谚语. Farmers' saying or old saw.

Yang Jingxian 杨景贤. Late Yuan - early Ming writer, author of *Journey to the West Variety Show* (*Xiyouji zaju* 西游记杂剧).

Yang Shen 杨慎 (1488–1559). Ming dynasty scholar and poet, author of *Obscure Allusions Used by the Art Circles*.

*yu* 竽. Traditional Chinese musical instrument with a dozen bamboo pipes on top of a bowl-like copper base.

Zhang Sengyao 张僧繇. Liang dynasty painter.

Zhang Yanyuan 张彦远 (815–907 CE). Tang dynasty painter and (China's first) art historian, author of *Famous Paintings of All the Past Dynasties*.

Zhuangzi 庄子 (c. 369–286 BCE), also known as Zhuangzhou 庄周. Warring States period Daoist philosopher.

*Zhuangzi* 庄子. Daoist classic written by the philosopher Zhuangzi.

# Dynasties of China

Xia 夏 and Shang 商 dynasty (semi-mythical) (2100-1045 BCE)
Zhou 周 dynasty (1045-256 BCE)
    Western Zhou 西周 (1045–771 BCE)
    Eastern Zhou 东周 (770–221 BCE)
Spring and Autumn period 春秋时代 (770–476 BCE)
Warring States period 战国时期 (475–221 BCE)
Qin 秦 dynasty (221–206 BCE)
Han 汉 dynasty (206 BCE –220 CE)
    Western Han 西汉 (206–25 CE)
    Eastern Han 东汉 (25–220 CE)
Three Kingdoms period 三国时代 (220–265 CE)
Jin 晋 dynasty (265–420 CE)
Southern and Northern Dynasties 南北朝 (420–589 CE)
    Liu Song 刘宋 Dynasty (420–479 CE)
Sui 隋 dynasty (581–618 CE)
Tang 唐 dynasty (618–907 CE)
Five Dynasties period 五代 (907–960 CE)
Song 宋 dynasty (960–1279)
Jurchen Jin 女真金 dynasty (1125–1234)
Yuan 元 dynasty (1279–1368)
Ming 明 dynasty (1368–1644)
Qing 清 dynasty (1644–1911/12)

www.ingramcontent.com/pod-product-compliance
Ingram Content Group UK Ltd.
Pitfield, Milton Keynes, MK11 3LW, UK
UKHW021313180426
11947UKWH00015B/1208